Practical Winning Strat

A guide to putting Sales and Ma
Software Business

By Terry Forsey

GW01403047

Published by Terry Forsey Consulting 2011

Contents

Introduction

When I started Terry Forsey Consulting in 2002 I had the vision of providing a complete Consultancy service to Software Businesses encompassing not just Sales and Marketing but integrating these disciplines into a holistic view of the business.

Since that time I have had the pleasure of working with a very large number of Software and Technology companies run by some very clever people. What I believe I can bring to their lives and businesses is my prior experience of working within smaller owner companies for over 25 years and my drive and determination to continue to master new ideas and innovative techniques to great effect.

When I started in January 2002 Google was not the market leading search engine and Google AdWords was being dismissed by many corporations as inferior to Banner Advertising. How the world has changed. I launched my first Marketing Campaign as a Direct Mail to a purchased database and within a few weeks I had my first five customers two of which are still clients! It became rapidly clear to me and my Client Base, if we were to punch more than our weight and compete effectively with the biggest players we would have to harness our nimbleness to maximum effect.

Taking some of my own medicine I stopped all direct mail and associated out bound traditional marketing and embraced the world of Websites, Google, AdWords, SEO and e-Marketing and sought to integrate these within mine and my clients businesses to achieve three goals.

1. To develop high performance management teams with clear vision and effective processes, leading to profitable growth.

2. To allow even the smallest business to compete with the largest competitor through highly effective marketing, placing the website at the centre of all activities.

3. To improve the way software was sold by focusing selling on the customer and their needs thus ensuring the delivery of maximum customer value through the sales process.

Over the last five years I have published a regular programme of white papers to help the Smaller Software Businesses start to achieve these goals. I am delighted to bring together a number of these ideas and thoughts into this publication "Practical Winning Strategies - A guide to putting Sales & Marketing at the heart of your Software Business"

In preparing this publication, I would like to thank all my Customers, Colleagues and Friends who have provided invaluable feedback and positive criticism on everything we do.

Chapter One
The Challenges of generating and converting leads

Buying is as much a process as any other business activity. Prospective customers gradually become active buyers. The buying cycle is effectively the way in which people behave when making a purchase. It should also determine the way your business interacts with the market and your customers.

Furthermore we need to understand know how a prospective customer selects their preferred software or service supplier.

This chapter focuses on a simple fact. If you are armed with a better knowledge the customer's buying and selection processes and integrate this knowledge into your selling activities then you can have a serious impact on your future success.

Chapter One
The Challenges of generating and converting leads

How Customers Buy?

We all spend a lot of time searching for prospective customers who are looking for our products or services, but do we ever stop to think about the transition from being a non-buyer to being a happy customer?

Buying is as much a process as any other business activity. Prospective customers don't suddenly become active buyers, it's a gradual process. Now here's the most interesting thing. If you can engage an organisation early in that process you stand three times more chance of winning them as a customer.

I know we can go on sales training courses, undertake marketing skills development but is there anything you can do that would increase your outcome by a factor of three? I would be amazed.

This paper is focused on the following simple fact. If you embrace this methodology and adopt the techniques then you can have a serious impact on your future success.

The Buying Cycle
The buying cycle is effectively the way in which people behave when making a purchase. It should also determine the way your business interacts with the market and your customers in order to help them move from being an inactive buyer to an active buyer who is happy to make a purchase.

Once we understand that process we can start to identify the techniques we can adopt to enhance our position within that process and increase our chances of converting potential buyers into customers.

You should be looking to attract customers into a long term relationship and enhance that relationship with existing customers too.

The idea is to capture potential customers as early in their individual buying cycle as possible via marketing and then to build a relationship which transcends any singular purchase. In turn, this ensures that you can benefit from the individual customers for years to come.

There are numerous opportunities for you to make contact with the customer. In fact, you should be aiming to achieve seven valuable contact points and it is your number one challenge and priority to deliver those incidences of contact throughout the buying lifecycle to convert inactive customers into active customers.

If you manage that then my research shows you can be up to **THREE TIMES** more likely to win them as a customer on a long term basis.

Chapter One
The Challenges of generating and converting leads

You will find more about the Seven Valuable Contacts Challenge in the white paper "Boost your sales in an economic downturn – Guaranteed!" (Chapter 2)

Let's start looking at the buying lifecycle and look at a buyer who is in a "Satisfied State".

Satisfied State
This is someone who is doing their job as part of their everyday activity. We are naturally creatures of habit and quickly settle into a routine. When we are satisfied we will rarely look to consider change in any way. The saying "if it ain't broke, don't fix it" sums up this stage best. The customer is not active in the buying lifecycle and does not explore options for change.

Sub-Consciously Dissatisfied
At this stage a buyer starts to become aware of alternative solutions. They are looking to be educated and start to realise that there are alternatives without spending much time thinking about them. The result is that current activities start to feel a bit "long-in-the-tooth". Aspects of what they do start to become quirky which grate on their nerves.

The buyer is inactive.
Communication from your company is marketing focused. A seller is unlikely to be involved.

Marketing communication should concentrate on education and seek to deliver materials that are valuable in their content.

Chapter One
The Challenges of generating and converting leads

Dissatisfied
The buyer has made a decision to do something to make a change and the transition from being inactive to active buyer begins.

Recognition of Need
The customer is developing detailed requirements here in order to find a product or service to fulfil all needs. The budget is assigned to fulfil the need. This is the stage at which people begin to actively look for a solution. Formalised project is underway with assessment and selection criteria being established.

Evaluate Options
The buyer and seller are now active. The competitive battlefield is uncovering the relevant critical issues. There is the potential for the first company in the frame to convert an active customer into a sale. Therefore you have to make sure that you are the first company to do so.

Evaluation of alternatives
Should your product leave any questions at all in the buyers mind then they will evaluate and compare other products and services with a view to finding out whether there is a better fit or a keener price. They will then undertake a detailed assessment of each option with a view of reaching a short list.

The later your organisation becomes involved the less chance you have of winning the sale. Your challenge is to be absolutely sure that your business is discovered as early in the active phase as possible, even better when the customer is in the inactive phase.

Resolution of Concerns
The buyer is at their most active in the process and has found the solution that they need.

Support offered
Marketing continues to support with education and supportive messages to ensure that the customer is fully satisfied with their decision and all needs are fulfilled. This should be ongoing to encourage a long term relationship where applicable.

Implementation Phase
This is where a decision is turned into reality. The buyer is no longer active they have made a decision in response to a problem. Unsuccessful sellers often try to reopen the decision but, as the customer's focus has moved, this tactic is rarely successful.

You will not be surprised to know that every salesman wants to find a buyer who is actively trying to understand what they are looking for and evaluating alternatives. That's their job.

Chapter One
The Challenges of generating and converting leads

Companies on the other hand should be looking to engage buyers and their colleagues when they are not active and possibly even at the satisfied state. This way you can start to deliver education and convey the strength of your message.

If you can deliver valuable communications, the first of your valuable contacts, then you are setting the agenda against which alternatives will be evaluated when the time is right. If you invested in building a relationship of value when the customer was not active what would your salesman say if they were **THREE TIMES** more likely to close a sale as a result?

Now that you understand a little about the buying life-cycle and the stages within it you will see that it is a continuous process and one that all buyers and customers will go through.

To harness the opportunities this presents then you need a website to play a fundamental role in the process to stand any chance of success at all.

Conclusion
So now you can see that buying is as much a process as any other business activity.

Prospective customers gradually become active buyers and if you can engage an organisation early in that process you stand three times more chance of winning them as a customer.

This section provides a methodology which if you embrace it and adopt the techniques can have a serious impact on your future success.

Chapter One
The Challenges of generating and converting leads

How Customer's select their Preferred Supplier?

We often think we know how a prospective customer selects their preferred software or service supplier but do we ever stop and test our assumptions?

Furthermore, have we stopped to think whether a first time buyer uses the same selection criteria as someone who is buying for a second or subsequent time?

Good questions and ones that should be answered by rigorous research not gut feeling or assumption.

At some stage when a company is growing they will be looking at their technology and asking the following questions,

"Is this adequate to cope with our growth plans?"
"Can we achieve productivity gains with our existing systems?"
"Are our business processes supported by our technology or a slave to it?"

It is the answer to these questions that drives companies to start to seek new systems and creates a purchasing project to select their preferred supplier.

This paper provides an insight into the decision criteria which drives customer's buying and selection behaviour.

The Deloitte and Touche market research

A few years ago Deloitte and Touche surveyed hundreds of companies who had recently purchased a new ERP system to understand the criteria they used in selecting their preferred supplier. What was unique about this survey is that they separated out the respondents' criteria into first time and second time purchasers to determine if experience changed purchasing criteria.

While these results are based on ERP systems the message can be applied to any significant software and service purchase project within similar organisations.

If you look at the experienced purchaser's (2nd time buyers) results below, support and track record were the top criteria while the first time purchasers had these near at the bottom.

Chapter One
The Challenges of generating and converting leads

Top 10 Criteria for Selecting Software	2nd Time	1st Time
1. Level of support from the solution provider	1	8
2. Vendor's track record of performance	2	10
3. Software's ability to fit the business	3	4
4. Growth potential of software	4	7
5. Price of the software	5	1
6. Quality of documentation	6	9
7. Functionality of the software	7	5
8. Ease of use	8	3
9. Ease of implementation of the new system	9	2
10. Software works with existing hardware	10	6

2nd Time Buyers
Level of support from the solution provider
Vendor's track record of performance
Software's ability to fit the business
Growth potential of software
Price of the software
Quality of documentation
Functionality of the software
Ease of use
Ease of implementation of the new system
Software works with existing hardware

1st Time Buyers
Price of the software
Ease of implementation of the new system
Ease of use
Software's ability to fit the business
Functionality of the software
Software works with existing hardware
Growth potential of software
Level of support from the solution provider
Quality of documentation
Vendor's track record of performance

This clearly demonstrates that experienced decision maker's value the supplier's expertise above all else while the inexperienced decision makers often don't understand how critical these abilities are to the implementation. Additionally, inexperienced purchasers put price as their top criteria yet experienced purchasers put price out of the top three criteria. So, experienced buyers look for software vendors that have experience,

Chapter One
The Challenges of generating and converting leads

understand business process and have a large stable of clients who see them as trusted advisors.

Ten steps the customer will take to evaluate each supplier

The first thing to be aware of here is that good buyers of software and services will be aware of surveys like the one mentioned above and will be gearing up to apply a number of tests to their potential suppliers.

Research all potential suppliers,
- Review their website,
- Do a Google search on their web presence.
- Undertake a Companies House Search

Check out their credentials,
- Are they qualified to sell any third party software?
- How long have they been in business?
- How long have they been selling these solutions?
- How strong are their partner relationships?
- How many people focus specifically on these solutions?

Check out their Customers,
- What is the geographic spread of their customers?
- Are you within that Geography?

Meet the "interview" the supplier,
- Are they compatible with us?
- Can we work together?
- Do they listen and demonstrate they understand our business and our needs?

What is their supply process?
- How do they gather our requirements?
- How do they manage
  - Customisation?
  - Implementation?
  - Training?
  - Technical Support?
  - Upgrades?
  - Maintenance?

Do they have adequate resources?
- Have they provided a project timeline for implementation?
- Can they demonstrate they have adequate resources?
- What are the skills and qualifications of the identified project staff?

Chapter One
The Challenges of generating and converting leads

Have we seen a presentation of our solution?
- This is not a selling demonstration but a presentation addressing our specific needs.

Are their prices clear?
- Is there a cost breakdown?
- Are they clear about what's included?
- How will they handle additional requests which are outside the scope of their pricing?

Check out their references
- Request references from similar companies (size, industry, number of employees, distance from their support centre etc.)
- Ask about implementation, support, people, good experiences, area of improvement etc.

Have they a clear value proposition
- How can we cost justify our investment?
- Has a value justification or Return on Investment model been provided to help our cost justification?

As a potential supplier you should likewise be aware of your potential customer's motivations and should be seeking to ensure you are equipped with the necessary information to compete most effectively.

The following questions are very likely to be asked by an experienced customer of their potential suppliers.

Conclusion
This section provides an insight into how a prospective customer selects their preferred software or service supplier based on rigorous research.

It distinguishes the different behaviour of the first time buyers from someone buying for a second or subsequent time.

Finally it provides a straightforward checklist of the ten tests a prospective customer will apply to competing suppliers. Armed with this information you can begin to fine tune your sales process enabling you to compete most effectively

Chapter One
The Challenges of generating and converting leads

Chapter Two
Improving sales effectiveness

Today, it's no longer what you sell, but how you market yourself that determines your success. Value no longer resides in the technology rather in the manner in which it is marketed. Adapting to these market conditions requires that everyone involved in selling should move beyond simply communicating what is inherent in a product or a technology. Instead they must provide insight to potential customers in terms of value that can't be found elsewhere.

Software businesses that create value beyond what is inherent in the product and deliver better, more measurable outcomes for their customers can fundamentally change the buyer/seller interaction.

Most prospects are not interested in what your products and services do or how they do it! **They only want to know what you can do for them.** If they determine that what you have will solve their problem, they will want to know how your particular product works, the features. Most salespeople honestly, and mistakenly, believe that prospects need to be educated before they can make an intelligent decision.

This chapter delivers one simple message - The way you sell can seriously differentiate your business. The results can be outstanding.

Chapter Two
Improving sales effectiveness

From Transactional Selling to Selling Solutions

There is no one 'style' of selling. Every business develops its own style often tied to the processes that grow up over many years. Some styles evolve and others remain stuck in the past with consequences for the company concerned. However all these various styles can be put into groups that can be loosely characterised as either Transactional Selling or Selling Solutions.

Over time selling has evolved. It used to be the FAB (Feature Advantage Benefit) approach which was in its day a considered and successful way of closing business. At the end of the 1990's this changed into the selling solutions approach.

Transactional selling was all about closing the order there and then and typically involved negotiation with the buyer on price with little interaction with others in the company. Therefore highly trained sales people were unable to use their well tuned sales techniques as they tended to be talking not to decision makers but influencers at best. (This is not true of all industries but it is certainly true of many.) In the transactional world there was limited competition and frequently the transactional sales person was termed, perhaps unfairly, as an order taker. This was in the good old days of a seller's market.

The move to selling solutions was created by the development of more and more competition, much more savvy buyers and the need to influence the decision makers at an earlier stage in the sales process.

Selling Solutions is the process of developing a comprehensive understanding of the customer's business and industry, defining needs at a strategic level and offering solutions that will help the customer address their unique objectives. We are not talking here about an old fashioned order taker. Here we need a different person who is more a business manager who has business as well as sales acumen.

In the modern era when products and services have to conform to standards and when numerous companies make almost identical products selling at the same price other differentiators come into play. The successful sales person understands that price alone is not the only criteria for decision making and will work closely with all decision makers and influencers to achieve their goals.

There is a clear difference in how you sell commodities as opposed to more complex products and services. Specific selling techniques and skill sets are required to be effective at selling either of them.

Chapter Two
Improving sales effectiveness

Customers today are more educated and less tolerant of sales jargon. They want suppliers who offer complete product and services and ones that develop new ideas year after year. They look to these vendors for help when solving secondary problems directly related to the product or service being purchased.

The bottom line is, when you want to create a competitive advantage, you have to offer a complete package. As a "total solutions provider," you separate yourself from your competition and position yourself to close larger sales.

In fact the way you sell can become in itself a significant differentiator for your company.

To make the transition from transactional to consultative selling, one must understand a few key concepts and terms.

Are you a supplier or a problem solver?
Salespeople that act as a supplier typically provide a commodity. They focus on one need at a time and are less aware of the customer's overall situation. Sales are made on a quantitative or volume basis. A problem solver provides solutions and adds value. They have a different skill set and are aware of the wider needs of the customer. They have a greater level of customer knowledge and satisfy several needs at once. Sales are made on a qualitative basis.

The difference between transactional and selling solutions
Transactional sales solve immediate customer needs and are typically short-term in nature. They require a shorter sales cycle with a specific means to an end. Selling Solutions opportunities are often broader in scope and may be trend driven. They address both the immediate and long-term needs of the client. The time frame for the "sale" is not finite and usually employs an on-going cycle. This type of sale often requires the collaboration of a number of people on both sides of the equation. There is a greater level of customer knowledge and an atmosphere of long-term relationship building.

Selling Solutions (also known as: strategic selling, relationship selling, complex selling, consultative selling and partnership selling).The customer is looking for Return on Investment information since the sale frequently represents a capital investment. Because of the size and complexity of the sale and the number of decision makers involved the sales cycle can be long. The relationship with the customer is paramount. This sounds cliché, but the salesperson is really selling a solution to the customer's perceived needs.

Information gathering can consume a substantial amount of time; questioning and listening skills are essential. The salesperson will be dealing with high level, if not Director Level, decision makers.

Transactional Selling (also known as: commodity selling and retail selling) Success in transactional sales is often primarily a result of raw sales activity. The primary role of the transactional salesperson is to swiftly match the customer's needs to a product or service.

Surprisingly, there have been studies that indicate that the top one percent of transactional salespeople earn more income than the top one percent of solution salespeople. Exceptional transactional sales professionals who can manage themselves and their time in order to sell enormous amounts of products and services are well compensated. The sales cycle for transactional sales is short.

What is the definition of price and value?
The purpose here is not to replace Wikipedia, rather to clarify two critical terms as they relate to the Selling solutions process.

- The price is what you pay for a product or service. It is the number attached to that product or service. It is well defined.
- The value is what you believe you receive for the price. It is a perception and is very subjective. It is not always quantifiable. Price invites competition. Value locks out the competition.

The Selling Solutions Approach
A well-defined Selling Solutions strategy will help you align your product or service with the customer's perception of value.

- It moves the sale away from price.
- This process should be designed to accomplish three things.
- The selling organization to position themselves as problem solvers and not as product peddlers.
- To secure larger and more frequent sales opportunities.
- To offer high margin products and/or services along with the ones that may be currently viewed as commodities.

Typically, the **Selling Solutions process will have three steps**.

The first is to establish a clear understanding of the customer's requirements, priorities and overall goals. This usually takes place at multiple levels within the customer's organisation and may require several meetings.

The second step is to identify areas you can improve in their current process. This may be specific problems you can solve, performance gaps to close or areas in which they want to grow. These opportunities are usually present because of deficiencies with the current vendor, the advent of new technologies or the customer's lack of knowledge in a particular area.

The third step is where you match the customer's priorities with the areas to improve and your offering or capabilities. This is called creating the value.
When taking the Selling Solutions approach, think of ways to provide the customer with a greater return on their investment. Quantify for them the

savings or gains in time, money and/or additional resources. This way you position yourself as a problem solver or consultant and not just another vendor. By doing so, you will create tremendous competitive advantages.

As the products and services that are available to businesses get more complex, the number of selling solutions professionals continues to grow. With the explosion of e-commerce the number of traditional transactional sales professionals continues to decline. Simply stated, the Internet is replacing many non-value-added order processors. All of this is good news for salespeople; there are an increasing number of more highly paid and rewarding Selling Solution jobs available.

Conclusion
Whether you are selling commodities in a transactional environment or selling complex services or products in a solutions based sales environment, it is essential that you use the appropriate and most effective selling techniques for what you are selling and to whom you are selling.

Too many salespeople get this mixed up and use transactional techniques with customers when they should be using relational techniques and vice versa. It is important to keep the sales environment in mind when hiring sales people. Moving a salesperson from one type of selling to another can be difficult and frustrating for everyone, especially if the salesperson has many years of experience in primarily one environment.

Chapter Two
Improving sales effectiveness

Boost your Sales in an economic downturn!

The Value of Building Seven Valuable Contacts

Introduction
Selling is as much an art as it is a science. Too often businesses focus on driving more and more new leads. In an economic downturn it may be difficult to generate new enquiries.

Too often you have under your nose sources of opportunity which will at some time definitely buy. It may not be today, it may not be next month but if they have a need then they will buy something, sometime.

This paper concentrates on improving the engagement with these opportunities and focused on improving your winning potential by building Seven Valuable Contacts with prospects.

There are no hard and fast rules to be applied rigidly rather principles to be considered for each sale and if you follow this strategy your success ratio will grow boosting your sales revenues!

That's guaranteed!

Section 1 - Background
Before we consider how to improve our engagement and the art of building Seven Valuable Contacts I wanted to consider two groups for whom, while their relationship with your business may be markedly different, the Seven Valuable Contacts principles can be equally applied.

Group 1- Customers won't decide
One of the common problems I hear from business managers is that they meet a prospective customer who is keen to do business. But often after a good meeting the sale stalls. Moving the deal along becomes a struggle. The salesman makes a number of follow up calls but soon becomes frustrated because either they have nothing fresh to say or they are being perceived to be pushy.

From the customer's perspective, they may struggle to explain the reasons for the purchase or find it difficult to sell the project internally.

The result on both sides is lack of progress and a difficulty to progress the project.

Section 2 looks at some techniques to help you maintain quality contact with these customers and reignite the sale.

Group 2 - Not enough leads

I meet a lot of good technology companies and I often have the conversation which goes something like this. "Our problem is that we cannot generate new leads. When we are face to face with a good prospect we stand our best chance of winning a new customer."

I am sure this is true of a large number of businesses.

Then when I start to dig a little I get some more information which starts to put some dimensions to the situation. I have yet to meet anyone who converts every face to face meeting into a new customer. More than often a meeting has one of four outcomes:

1. A broad enquiry where there's some interest but not just yet. The prospect is gathering information and, as and when there are good and ready, they may do something.
2. A genuine interest and they are keen on an alternative solution.
3. A genuine interest and you are the preferred choice.
4. No interest for a variety of reasons.

For each business the proportion of meetings across these groups varies but it is rare that a positive result is achieved in the majority of situations.

So to conclude in my experience over 50% of people you meet do not buy from you.

Some buy from someone else but are these always satisfied customers? They may be unhappy with the choice they have made but do they return to talk to you?

Some decide to just limp along with their existing relationship. Often people find it difficult to re-open a dialogue with a "rejected supplier", only making a change when a new supplier engages with them.

Some may not be quite ready to buy and when they are, they are ready to reconsider who to buy from.

Some do not buy at all. Hence you have a significant competitor out there called customer apathy.

Now before you invest yet more time and money chasing after new leads let's stop and think about how many people you have spoken to in the last three years. Do you have contact details of all these people? How often have you contacted them?

Read on to discover how you can reignite these relationships.

Section 2 - Reignite deals with Seven Valuable Contacts

Established wisdom says that, "on average", you need to make Seven Valuable Contacts with a prospect to convert their initial interest into a signed up customer.

Now it is reasonable to assume that if you had a positive first meeting then that constitutes a valuable contact. If that is not the case then there is no real opportunity for you.

To take this initial interest and engineer a sale you need "on average" six more valuable contacts. I must emphasise here that sometimes deals happen quickly and require less than Seven Valuable Contacts. But if you don't persevere and work at your personal "average" you will be losing deals which will buy and, if you demonstrate determination, could happily buy from you. This inevitably means that some deals will require a higher level of valuable contact than seven.

Now there is one important component in this equation. That is the word "valuable". To achieve Seven Valuable Contacts the judgement of the value is solely with the recipient – the potential customer. If they do not perceive the contact to have been of value it fails!

It doesn't matter how well prepared your script, how creative your brochure or how engaging your PowerPoint. If your prospect does not think it's of value then IT'S NOT!

Calling to ask if they've reviewed your proposal is unlikely to be considered valuable – no matter how well rehearsed your objection handling!

To get you thinking and to help achieve the magical Seven Valuable Contacts here are some ideas you may consider when striving for your Seven Valuable Contacts.

Follow up communication - After a good meeting with a prospective customer it is often very valuable for both parties if the seller writes as a follow up. While this can be an email or a traditional letter it is most important that this communication is valuable to the customer.

A valuable follow up letter needs to demonstrate that you the seller have a clear view as to the reason why the customer wants to work with you. What is their need? If you answer the following five questions in this letter it will be of great value to the customer.

1. What is their real driving need or "critical issue"? What is the problem you can solve?
2. What are the impacts of this problem across their organisation?
3. What vision does the customer have of a potential solution to their problem?
4. How can you solve the customer's problem?

5.   How can you prove that your solution is best?

Presentation - Presentations can be a double edged sword. They can be very powerful or an outright turnoff. To ensure your presentation is perceived to be of value, avoid "standard" PowerPoint slides which talk about who you are and what you do.

Instead make your presentation personal to the customer. Focus on what you can do for their business. Show them how they can use your product or service in their world.

Customer Contact – Many prospective customers would like to know what it's really like working with your product or your service. Testimonials can really help establish your credentials and credibility but there's nothing like real customer contact.

Don't wait for a prospect to ask if they could speak to an existing customer, plan for it. Offer to introduce them to a similar organisation who they can speak to. Not only is such an offer valuable it's also shows confidence and enthusiasm in what you do.

Don't be surprised if your confidence and enthusiasm means that your prospective customer does not make that call!

Technical Contact - Very often a more technical solution may require an in depth technical assessment. Technical conversations often involve different contacts both within the customer's organisation and within yours.

It is a very powerful message to let the technical contact take place in your absence. It shows great confidence in the abilities of your colleagues. After all you won't always be there to deliver after sales service. It also provides an opportunity to reconvene in a subsequent meeting to review the effectiveness of the technical contact and address any resulting issues.

References and Case Studies - To be successful selling you need to earn the trust of a customer and together you can work to solve their problem. To be able to start earning trust and be deemed trustworthy you need to prove your ability not brag about it.

Reference stories have been designed to enable you to talk about successful customer projects. A full Customer Case Study can often be time consuming and expensive to produce.

Proposal or Quotation – If at all possible avoid issuing a simple quotation rather prepare a personalised proposal. There are four categories of content that proposals must contain to maximise your chance of winning:

Chapter Two
Improving sales effectiveness

- Evidence you understand the customer's problem.
- A recommendation for a specific solution that will solve the problem and produce positive business results.
- A compelling reason for the client to choose your recommendation over any others.
- Evidence of your ability to deliver – the proof of concept.

News Clippings – As you browse newspapers, magazines, websites you will often see material of interest to you and your customers. Send a copy to a relevant prospective customer with an appropriate note. It shows you are interested in them as a customer.

Relevant Industry Information – This is a more extensive collection of materials than just news clippings. It would include industry white papers, brochures, advertisements, product literature, websites etc. In this online publication ages there is a magnitude of information available online.

White Papers – White papers can be a very valuable source of information to customers and prospective customers. Just as with this document listen to your customers and prepare materials which interest, educate and, most importantly, are perceived to be of value!

Newsletter - To be sure that your newsletter is well received it needs to include content of value to the reader. Recruiting a new office manager or moving offices may not be valuable to most readers.

To be sure you are really delivering value you will need to research to understand the needs of your market. Monitor and review this regularly.

If you choose to make you newsletter electronic ensure you have the tools to monitor interest levels on "click-throughs". This is important information to help you know what really interests readers.

How often should you produce a newsletter? To keep your company in the mind of the reader and to move towards Seven Valuable Contacts then monthly is considered to be best. If you are unable to produce a monthly newsletter then make it quarterly.

Most important always deliver on time and avoid slippages.

Social Contact – This can be anything from a cup of coffee or a pie and a pint to attending a football match or a round of golf. Social contact will have two dimensions.

The first providing an opportunity to get to know each other, helping your prospective customer know what you're like
Social contact also provides an informal environment to touch on any business related issues which may need addressing.

Chapter Two
Improving sales effectiveness

Summary

There are no hard and fast rules you can apply to get success on every occasion. Each sale is different and needs to be thought through to determine the right valuable contact at each stage.

What is absolutely true is that if you follow this strategy and try to exceed Seven Valuable Contacts for each sale then your success ratio is guaranteed to grow boosting your sales revenues!

Chapter Two
Improving sales effectiveness

Boost your revenues today by re-awakening stalled sales opportunities

How many stalled prospective deals do you have clogging your pipeline? What if you could re-awaken them, or better yet, avoid these stalls in the first place?

You believe you have done everything right: Your prospect has clearly explained their business and relevant personal issues. You feel you have connected to those issues with the solution you can provide. You are working directly with the person who has the authority and ability to make the decision. You've agreed, in writing, what you and the prospect will do together to initiate a business relationship. The only thing that you haven't been able to do is get them to sign on the dotted line.

Unfortunately, like most salespeople, between 30 and 50 percent of the sales in your pipeline will result in no decision. In a tough market, one of the biggest productivity returns you can reap is to reduce the impact of stalled decisions by identifying them early in the sales cycle. However, in order to reawaken a stalled sale, you must first diagnose the reasons behind it. The problem isn't always that the sale has stalled. The problem is that often we don't recognise it soon enough and expend time and resources on these dead-end opportunities.

One of the most common questions I hear from clients has to do with stalled opportunities. The scenario typically goes something like this: a sales cycle is progressing with an individual - all the buying signals are there - and then ... nothing happens! No return phone calls, no return emails and no communication at all! What do you do?

After reviewing hundreds of stalled sales cycles over the years, I have identified the seven most common explanations for a sale in limbo.

1. Lack of connection to a critical business issue
Many software salespeople are fascinated with the features and benefits of their products and services.

Most prospects are not interested in what your products and service do or how they do it! They only want to know what you can do for them. If they determine that what you have will solve their problem, they will want to know how your particular product works, the features. Most salespeople honestly, and mistakenly, believe that prospects need to be educated before they can make an intelligent decision.

Unless your solution addresses a serious business issue such as increased revenue, time to market, cost management, improved quality, competitive differentiation, better decision making or some other looming business issue tied to it, you can expect a stall. Senior executives only spend time on matters that directly impact their business.

Chapter Two
Improving sales effectiveness

There are only three questions a salesman has to ask to uncover business issues:
1. Why do you want this solution?
2. Why are those problems important to solve?
3. Why would that matter to you or any other executive in the company?

2. Lack of perceived value
Most people can only juggle six or seven critical issues at a time.

We prioritise issues in order of their importance or "value" - the benefit tied to solving the issue. If value isn't identified, an issue will quickly fall off of the list and be given no further attention.

For each deal in your pipeline, can your prospect articulate the "value" or impact of addressing this business issue? If your solution, from their perspective, doesn't have enough value to get in the top seven issues, you'll be put on the back burner.

So when meeting with a prospect, explore the impact of resolving the business issue. Ask probing questions and better still, ask how the solution will impact them personally.

I recently met a company that had recruited two new salesmen. They give them their sales literature and told them to "Say these things" on the phone. Then they call and recite phrases like, "We unfold the technology of tomorrow, today." Oh, now do I have a clear picture of how that will help me. Definitely not!

The fact is, most "benefits" are not. That's because, most "benefit" statements are not descriptions of results for the prospect. They talk about products, services, and slogans, and, a benefit is only a benefit if the person hearing it perceives it as one at that very moment.

Leave no doubt about what you can do for the prospect.

Analyse your own "benefit" statements. Put yourself in the position of your prospects. If you heard those statements would you be able to say "So what?" Or, would there be no doubt as to the results you might get. And THAT is what makes it a benefit.

3. Lack of any urgency
If a prospect delays making a decision it may be they're struggling to decide or they have no imperative to make a quick decision.
a) Lack of differentiation
Lack of differentiation will cause the prospect to spend more time evaluating alternatives, sometimes going into minute detail. The net effect is that this translates into a stall.

If you can link your product or service to real business issues for the prospect you can avoid delays. But if you are unable to differentiate your solution on capabilities and abilities to solve problems, you will be forced to differentiate on price.

b) Create deadlines or incentives to buy
People have become accustomed to acting under pressure and reacting in crisis. It may be that your buyers cannot decide until there's a deadline. If this is the case, create a reason to decide by a certain date. Offer a bonus that's only available for a couple of weeks. Mention the benefit of booking training dates for managers but only if a contract is signed in time to make the training arrangements by the end of the month.

c) Limit Choices to the important few instead of the meaningless many. Don't let trivial decisions overwhelm the prospect. This will overload them so that they're tempted to pull the plug on the whole project. Arrange all the details of your most popular choices into Plan A, Plan B, and Plan C choices. Offer those options as packages so the prospect doesn't have to tackle them step by step, decision by decision.

4. Make your proposal sell
Proposal writing may not be fun but winning a sale really is! From experience there are three reasons why a proposal can really help the salesman win business
1. A well thought out proposal can set the agenda for the sale
2. The way you sell can seriously differentiate yourself
3. In your absence, the proposal can "Do the selling" for you.

Your objective in writing a proposal is to provide your client with enough information, persuasively presented, to prove your case and motivate the client to buy your services or applications. That sounds pretty straightforward.

So why do the vast majority of proposals start with the company's history? Does the author believe there is something so fundamentally compelling about their origins that client will immediately be persuaded to buy?

And why do a huge number of proposals focus entirely on the company's products and services, but never mention how those products and services will help the client solve a business problem?
Does the proposal writer believe that facts alone are enough to motivate a prospect to say "yes"?

Winning proposals should be client centred, not company or product centred. Most people buy because they're looking for solutions to pressing problems, or the means to cope with difficult issues. What this means is that a proposal is not a price quote, a bill of materials, or a project plan. Each of those elements may be part of a proposal, but they are not sufficient to make a persuasive, client-centred case.

Chapter Two
Improving sales effectiveness

From experience, there are four categories of content that proposals must contain to maximise your chance of winning:

5. Lack of Clarity
The single biggest failing in most salespeople is that they are unable to describe their product or service clearly and briefly enough.

Most people take 20 to 30 seconds to decide whether they want what the sales person is selling. Prospects get frustrated and annoyed at the sales person who does not communicate with immediate clarity.

An effective prospecting offer should ideally be about 45 words. It takes many top sales people about two hours to design an effective and concise prospecting offer. Most sales people do not even know where to start.

Let me give you a dramatic example. A friend of mine recently received a voicemail from a sales representative which ran like this;
'The purpose of my call today is to introduce myself and take a moment to briefly describe for you two core-based technologies; laser Internet on-line office and an Internet broadcasting technology. I don't know whether or not any of these applications may be of interest to you, I would appreciate a brief moment of your time to review that.'
Were they of interest to him? He didn't know. He simply used technology for his business and only uses technology when he understands the value of what it enables him to do.

He would explain to his IT consultant what he wanted to accomplish and ask for his recommendations, in very plain English.

From the above message, he had no idea what 'core-based technologies' and 'laser internet on-line office,' meant. He had a sense of what 'an internet broadcasting technology' might be, but didn't know or understand its value to his business.

And that is the heart of the matter: What is the value? There was nothing in this message that enabled anyone to understand the value he had to offer. There was, therefore, no reason to return the call.

6. Proof
In high-tech sales, a common mistake is to deal with prospects on the basis of specifications, good presentations, logical arguments, convincing documentation, and factual economic justifications.
Most prospects, including engineers and senior managers, have different motives. Their first priority is to deal with a sales person that they fully trust and respect.

Only the top one percent of salesmen know how to establish that kind of relationship in the first half hour of meeting their prospects, and to continuously reinforce it.

Chapter Two
Improving sales effectiveness

What is "proof?"
Proof is when someone, other than you or your company, says something about your product, company, or service.

Proof includes letters of recommendation from other customers, testimonials, case studies, lists of clients, third party studies, copies of articles from trade journals, photographs of other customers using your product or service etc.

Anything you can find that in any way adds substance by someone else, even if it is remote and only distantly connected to your offer, will go a long way to supplying proof and helping build trust and respect.

7. Risk
Selecting a new supplier or a new solution involves risk for your prospect. The prospect's perception of risk can span business impacts, such as lost time or money; or personal ramifications, such as career or reputation. As a prospect gets closer to making a decision, the risk becomes greater in his mind.

Common tools for alleviating risk include supplying references, reinforcing vendor credentials, offering trial usage and demonstrating credibility with iron clad implementation plans, guarantees and your executive backing.

The concept of risk and its role in the buyer's mind is one of the most powerful concepts in the world of business-to-business sales. Taking it into account and planning to reduce the risk of every decision will be one of your most powerful sales strategies.

Offer evidence
Create opportunities for a prospect to touch, see, feel, and experience your product or service. Provide all the possible evidence of results. Put an indecisive prospect in touch with references who can offer assurances. Help them by delaying payment options until the prospect has an opportunity to "sample" your service and trust that you will not deliver and then run and hide.

Risk is several things. First, it is often the number one issue in the mind of the customer, particularly when the account has no history with your company. That makes it the number one issue to address in the sales process.

Risk is what the customer perceives it to be. In other words, it is not anything quantifiable, like the price or delivery of your offer. It is not objective or tangible. Instead it is much more insidious, lurking underneath almost every conversation between you and your customer. Because risk rises out of fear, risk is often not mentioned. To acknowledge risk is to admit fear. To admit fear is, in many people's minds, to expose weaknesses. No one wants to look weak.

Chapter Two
Improving sales effectiveness

Develop a closer personal relationship
The greater the relationship between buyer and the salesmen, the less the perceived risk.

That is why a prospect would prefer to buy a less effective product at a higher price from the sales person who has been calling on them for years. Focus, not on reducing the price, but rather in increasing the relationship.

Make the deal tangible
The more vague and intangible the purchase, the more risky the decision. Take all the imagination out of the buy. Bring prospects to your offices so they can see that you really do have a production facility. Take them to a location where the solution is being used by someone else. Hand them certificates of warranty instead of just telling them. Show them pictures of the product being used.

Look at every aspect of your offer, and think about how you can make this piece more tangible and objective.

Ask yourself, "Why the indecision?"
Buyers may stall at the point of decision for any number of reasons. Your response, of course, will depend on the reason:
Reason: They can't decide about the product or service.
Response: Offer more evidence and proof.

Reason: They can't decide about you or your organization.
Response: Increase credibility.

Reason: They can't determine how the decision might go over inside a "down" internal climate.
Response: Help them gather input or show value in a negative climate.

Reason: They are posturing for a price discount.
Response: Wait.

Reason: The answer is no and they're too timid to tell you.
Response: Ask point blank and give them permission to be straightforward with you.

Conclusion
Once you identify the likely cause of your stall, you can craft a strategy to reawaken your sales cycle by focusing on the missing link or underdeveloped component.

Equally important, with this new approach you can ensure that, in future, you avoid such stalls in the first place!
An easy way of calculating the risk is to ask yourself what happens to that individual if you or your company, mess up.

Hopefully, you now have a different perspective on your prospect. Your pricing is attractive, your product is better, your net impact on the customer will be positive, but they won't buy. It is not about the price, it is not about the quality, and it is not about the service. It is all about the risk!

If the risk to that person is high, the way to make the sale is to reduce that risk.

Here are three strategies for reducing the risk.

1. Offer evidence
Create opportunities for a prospect to touch, see, feel, and experience your product or service. Provide all the possible evidence of results. Put an indecisive prospect in touch with references who can offer assurances. Help them by delaying payment options until the prospect has an opportunity to "sample" your service and trust that you will not deliver and then run and hide.

Risk is several things. It is often the number one issue in the mind of the customer, particularly when the account has no history with your company. That makes it the number one issue to address in the sales process.

2. Develop a closer personal relationship
The greater the relationship between buyer and the salesmen, the less the perceived risk.

That is why a prospect would prefer to buy a less effective product at a higher price from the salesperson who has been calling on them for years. Focus, not on reducing the price, but rather in increasing the relationship.

3. Make the deal tangible
The more vague and intangible the purchase, the more risky the decision. Take all the imagination out of the buy. Bring prospects to your offices so they can see that you really do have a production facility. Take them to a location where the solution is being used by someone else. Hand them certificates of warranty instead of just telling them. Show them pictures of the product being used.

Look at every aspect of your offer, and think about how you can make this piece more tangible and objective.

The Power of Proof
Proof is when someone, other than you or your company, says something about your product, company, or service. Proof includes letters of recommendation from other customers, testimonials, case studies, lists of clients, third party studies, copies of articles from trade journals, photographs of other customers using your product or service etc. Anything you can find that in any way adds substance by someone else, even if it is remote and

only distantly connected to your offer, will go a long way to supplying proof and helping build trust and respect.

When we write proposals or make sales presentations, we typically try to establish the superiority of our recommendations by offering some kind of proof. In the world we work in, there are four kinds of proof we can offer to a prospect: the things we say about ourselves, the things our clients say about us, the things third-party, outside experts say, and the documented experience we can point to. Let's consider each of these, because they all have their own strengths and pitfalls.

Things we say about ourselves.
Every proposal contains some of these statements. "Our software is designed to be easy to learn and user friendly." "We are passionate about customer satisfaction." "We are a leader in developing effective treatment regimens." And so on.

Do they work? Actually, not all that well. Customers and prospects are likely to be sceptical of claims we make after all, why wouldn't we say positive things about ourselves? The other problem is we often lapse into clichés to communicate these claims-"best of breed products" combined with "state of the art implementation" and "world class support" producing "synergy and partnership" that results in "bottom line impact."

The best way to put some teeth in these claims is to ditch the clichés and back up each assertion with a bit of proof. For example, instead of saying we offer "best of breed products," why not say "we offer products from the seven largest manufacturers of moulding equipment, including three products that received the coveted 'injection moulding machine of the year' award."

Things our clients say about us.
These claims, which typically take the form of quotes, references, and testimonials, are more compelling. After all, your clients don't have to say anything at all. The fact that they're willing to do it is impressive.

The strongest way to buttress the value of quotes, references, and testimonials is to acknowledge that people are more comfortable listening to and believing what they hear from people who are similar to themselves. As a result, the best client proof statements will come from clients who are in the same industry, and who had similar challenges and got them resolved by working with you.

Third-party proof. Another source of influence is the phenomenon of "submission to authority". Perceived authority carries tremendous inherent persuasive power. As a result, if you can cite an outside source--a governing body, a recognized expert, or some other authority--it can have a strong impact on prospective customers. Similarly, if you've won awards, achieved a difficult status in your field, or had your excellence certified by a third-party agency, it's very much to your advantage to cite that proof.

The problem, of course, is that every industry has its "experts for hire," who will evaluate your product and rate it, partly based on how many of their publications you subscribe to at outrageous fees. This whole field is about as open and honest as figure skating competitions used to be. So, once again, a shiny endorsement from some group of experts may provoke yet another bout of scepticism in the prospect. But not always. And when it does, the scepticism is likely to be much lighter.

Documented experience. One of the best kinds of proof is the case study or a write up past performance. One reason they work so well is the fact that they often combine all three of the previous forms of proof statement into one concise package. You describe work you successfully accomplished for another client, quoting that client if possible, and citing figures showing the positive impact your work had on the client's organisation. You also mention any awards or recognition you received as a result of this work.

To maximize the impact of case studies or past performance write ups, keep them brief and organise them in terms of three general topics: the problem the client faced; the work you did; and the results they achieved. Avoid discussing previous work chronologically. Chronological structure creates wordiness and undercuts the impact of your real point.

Integrate Proof with your Seven Valuable Contacts
Established wisdom says that, "on average" you need to make Seven Valuable Contacts with a prospect to convert their initial interest into a signed up customer.

Now it is reasonable to assume that if you had a positive first meeting then that constitutes a valuable contact. If that is not the case then there is no real opportunity for you.

To take this initial interest and engineer a sale you need "on average" six more valuable contacts. I must emphasise here that sometimes deals happen quickly and require less than Seven Valuable Contacts. But if you don't persevere and work at your personal "average" you will be losing deals which will buy and, if you demonstrate determination, could happily buy from you. This inevitably means that some deals will require a higher level of valuable contact than seven.

Now there is one important component in this equation. That is the word "valuable". To achieve Seven Valuable Contacts the judgement of the value is solely with the recipient – the potential customer. If they do not perceive the contact to have been of value it fails! So calling to ask if they've reviewed your proposal is unlikely to be considered valuable.

To get you thinking and to help achieve the magical Seven Valuable Contacts here are some ideas you may consider when striving to deliver proof as part of your Seven Valuable Contacts.

References and Case Studies - To be successful selling you need to earn the trust of a customer and together you can work to solve their problem. To be able to start earning trust and be deemed trustworthy you need to prove your ability not brag about it.

Reference stories have been designed to enable you to talk about successful customer projects. A full Customer Case Study can often be time consuming & expensive to produce.

Proposal or Quotation – If at all possible avoid issuing a simple quotation rather prepare a personalised proposal. There are four categories of content that proposals must contain to maximise your chance of winning:

- Evidence you understand the customer's problem.
- A recommendation for a specific solution that will solve the problem and produce positive business results.
- A compelling reason for the client to choose your recommendation over any others.
- Evidence of your ability to deliver – the proof of concept.

News Clippings – As you browse newspapers, magazines, websites you will often see material of interest to you and your customers. Send a copy to a relevant prospective customer with an appropriate note. It shows you are interest in them as a customer.

White Papers – White papers can be a very valuable source of information to customers and prospective customers. Just as with this document listen to your customers and prepare materials which interest, educate and, most importantly, are perceived to be of value!

Newsletter - To be sure that your newsletter is well received it needs to include content of value to the reader. Recruiting a new office manager or moving offices may not be valuable to most readers.

To be sure you are really delivering value you will need to research to understand the needs of your market. Monitor and review this regularly.

If you choose to make you newsletter electronic ensure you have the tools to monitor interest levels on "click-through". This is important information to help you know what really interests readers.

How often should you produce a newsletter? To keep your company in the mind of the reader and to move towards Seven Valuable Contacts then monthly is considered to be best. If you are unable to produce a monthly newsletter then make it quarterly.

Most important always deliver on time and avoid slippages.

Chapter Two
Improving sales effectiveness

There are no hard and fast rules you can apply to get success on every occasion. Each sale is different and needs to be thought through to determine the right valuable contact at each stage.

What is absolutely true is that if you follow this strategy and try to exceed Seven Valuable Contacts for each sale you will deliver strong proof, minimise risk and your success ratio will grow, boosting your sales revenues.

Chapter Two
Improving sales effectiveness

Five critical questions to improve your sales success

There are lots of consultative sales methods focused on selling solutions. You may have been trained in one, or read a book about one that you particularly like.

Each has its own strengths and techniques. They all have at least one thing in common. They try to help sales people to focus on what matters to the customer. You build sales momentum by demonstrating that you are delivering an important solution to an important problem.

That is the essence of all these consultative Methodologies - to sell solutions.

To be able to create a client-centred solution - and to be able to write a client-centred proposal - there are five questions you must be able to answer.

Many people try to write proposals without knowing the answers to even half of these questions. That makes it impossible to create a message that sounds "right" to the buyer.

Here are the five questions. Make sure your sales people uncover the answers, make sure every proposal and sales presentation is based on them, and you'll win a lot more business.

1. What is the client's problem?
This is their PAIN. Look beyond the obvious. Your contact in the customer organisation may describe the problem in terms that are specific to his or her interests. An IT manager sees the lack of on-line access to customer account information as a data integrity problem.

To the Sales Director, it's a revenue problem, because it's keeping the sales force from separating good clients from the not so good.

If you have truly understood your customer's pain you should be able to say "Your critical issue is....." and the customer will instantly agree!

2. What are the impacts of problem?
- Why is the Critical Issue a problem?
- Who is affected by this problem?
- How are they affected?

Try to trace the links as high up the organisational ladder as possible to get a sense of how big the pain is. This will also indicate who else may need to be part of the decision team.

3. What vision does the client have of a successful solution?
- What does this customer think they need?
- How will they measure success?

- In terms of business or financial performance?
- In terms of improvements in the technology infrastructure?
- Or in terms of customer loyalty or employee morale?

Each of these areas - business results, technical outcomes, and social relationships - is potentially important.

Which leads us to the next question: They may all be important, but which measure matters the most? Which one really addresses the Critical Issue?

This tells you two things: First, it tells you the order in which to put your presentation of key outcomes. You want to put the customer's most important outcome first. That way, the customer will think that you think the way they think.

Second, knowing which issue is most important tells you where to look to develop your value proposition. You want to base your ROI or other presentation of value on what matters the most to the customer.

4. How can we solve the client's critical issue?
Usually there's more than one way to solve a particular problem. What is important is in presenting your solution to the customer's critical issue you are credible. Show them you truly understand their pain (Your critical issue is...) and demonstrate you understand the impacts.

Your solution should clearly show how you will both address the pain and justify recommendation. Your credibility will be clear from this understanding and when supported by testimonials, case studies and a clear ROI justification.

5. Why is our solution best?
Any of the potential solutions might take care of the problem. The important issue is what kind of outcome the customer will get. Will it match up to their expectations for a positive result? Will it meet their criteria?

Based on the answers to these, we should be able to answer the final question. It should be fairly obvious which solution meets the needs and delivers the results the customer desires most.

Trying to write a proposal or make a sales presentation without knowing the answers to these questions is like competing in an archery contest blindfolded. You might hit the bull's eye occasionally. But you're just as likely to shoot yourself in the foot.

Minimising Risk & Building Proof into your Sales Proposition

Chapter Two
Improving sales effectiveness

Selling is as much an art as it is a science. Too often businesses focus on driving more and more new leads without concentrating on the prospect's buying and decision making process.

One of the common problems I hear from business managers is that they meet a prospective customer who is keen to do business. But often after a good meeting the sale stalls. Moving the deal along becomes a struggle.

From the customer's perspective, they may struggle to explain the reasons for the purchase or find it difficult to sell the project internally.

The result on both sides is lack of progress and a difficulty to progress the project.

The indecisive buyer may or may not be a powerless tiger or political misfit, but the result to you proves to be the same: meeting after meeting; phone conversation after conversation; request after request for more information, proposals, pricing breakdowns, references, and evidence of results. And still no decision.

This paper explains how to help a prospective customer to understand the risk of doing business. It identifies the strategies to adopt to minimise the risk of your bid, helping you win more business. Furthermore it shows how to build proof into your sales process as an integral part of helping minimise the risk inherent in your bid.

Adopting these risk management and proof delivery strategies will dramatically improve the effectiveness of your sales process.

Risk assessment is a significant stage in decision making.
Selecting a new supplier or a new solution involves risk for your prospect. The prospect's perception of risk can span business impacts, such as lost time or money; or personal ramifications, such as career or reputation. As a prospect gets closer to making a decision, the risk becomes greater in his mind.

Common tools for alleviating risk include supplying references, reinforcing vendor credentials, offering trial usage and demonstrating credibility with iron clad implementation plans, guarantees and your executive backing.

The concept of risk and its role in the buyer's mind is one of the most powerful concepts in the world of business-to-business sales. Taking it into account and planning to reduce the risk of every decision will be one of your most powerful sales strategies.
Ask yourself, "Why the indecision?"
Buyers may stall at the point of decision for any number of reasons. Your response, of course, will depend on the reason:
- They can't decide about the product or service.

- They can't decide about you or your organization.
- They can't determine how the decision might go over inside a "down" internal climate.
- They are posturing for a price discount.
- The answer is no and they're too timid to tell you.
- The answer is proof.

Delivering proof through evidence will increase your credibility to help demonstrate value regardless of the economic climate.

Risk Minimisation the strategy to win the sale

Risk is several things. It is often the number one issue in the mind of the customer, particularly when the organisation has no history with your company. That makes it the number one issue to address in the sales process.

Sometimes it can be so frustrating. You know you have a better product or service than your prospect is currently using. Your price is attractive, your service is outstanding. If the prospect would switch to your solution, you know they would be delighted. You would save them money, smooth out their processes, reduce their inventory and generally make their life simpler.

So, why will they not switch? Are people really that stupid? Or, is it you? Did you do something to put them off?

While there are some circumstances where the answers would be yes to the questions above, the most likely answer is something totally different. The reason they will not switch is likely not their IQ, nor your deodorant. It is the risk!

Risk is a perception - what the customer perceives it to be. In other words, it is not quantifiable, like the price or delivery of your offer. Far from being objective or tangible it is totally intangible, lurking underneath almost every conversation between you and your customer. Risk rises out of fear and is often not mentioned. To acknowledge risk is to admit fear. To admit fear is, in many people's minds, to expose weaknesses. No one wants to look weak.

Risk is the answer to these two questions:
- What happens to the company if they make the wrong decision, how much risk do they accept when they say yes to you?
- What happens to the individual who is making the decision, if they make the wrong decision?

Risk is a combination of the financial, social, emotional, and time costs that the company and the individual decision-maker will bear as a result of making a mistake.

The Do's and Don'ts of writing a winning proposal.

Chapter Two
Improving sales effectiveness

These tips have been designed to help you focus on the priorities of writing successful and winning sales proposals.

The Do's
Focus on your customers' business needs or primary objectives first. Mirror what you have heard from them before offering a solution. This ensures you address what they care about most and shows that you've listened and considered their interests and are not offering a "one size fits all" approach.

Keep your proposal as short as possible. A short proposal is likely to be looked at first, which means all others will be judged in comparison to yours. That's a major advantage if you've done a good job.

Highlight your key points. Executives skim. You can improve the "skimability" of your proposal by highlighting key areas,
- using bullet points,
- graphics,
- pictures and
- Anything else that will make an impact and enable rapid reading.

Quantify your benefits and payback. Link these tightly to the customers' critical issues. Show the decision maker
- What they will achieve,
- How much they will save,
- How much more productive they can become.
- A convincing return on investment calculation is the most valuable payback.

Prioritise your unique factors and competitive advantages. Think about what you have to offer and select the strongest qualities and prioritise them in terms of what your customer's cares about. Where possible tie them into the payback calculation.

Ghost the competition. If you know who you are competing against, raise the issues in your proposal that strikes at their weak points.

Ask for the business. Ask in the covering letter. Ask for it in the executive summary. Ask for it when you deliver or present the proposal. Being passive sends out a weak signal – asking for the business send a most positive one.

The Don'ts
Never title your proposal "Proposal". That doesn't say anything to your customer that they don't know already. Would you ever title a book "Book"? Instead give it a title that states the benefit to the customer "Reducing costs through automation within the sales office."

Chapter Two
Improving sales effectiveness

Avoid lengthy corporate histories. Nobody's interested!

Don't use jargon. Even if you contact within your customer understands everything, who else will be reading and considering your proposal. Can you be sure they'll understand it? However it is all right to use the customer's own jargon, that's mirroring what you've heard.

Don't be tempted to throw in everything that might be of interest. In reality decision makers won't have time to read it. At best they'll skim through it.

Don't disparage the competition or mention them by name. But if you know their software is unstable or their support is poor, make a big deal about the importance of software reliability and quality of support.

Don't be a hard closer. Focus on the content of the proposal and ask for the business. You don't need strong-arm tactics. If you really solved the customers problem just ask for the business.

Don't use boilerplate messages. They're worse than no message at all. They sound canned and undercut any rapport you've created with the customer.

No one buys my Software!

Chapter Two
Improving sales effectiveness

Many small Software businesses will fail to achieve success in today's economy because they do not fully understand their customers' needs. This may be a hard hitting 'home truth' but I see this problem time and time again.

A common misunderstanding, and one quite difficult to grasp, is that customers do not actually buy your software or your service. No one buys Document Management or Batch Traceability. No one buys consulting services. No one buys ERP or CRM. In reality, customers purchase a solution to a problem.

You don't buy a hammer because you just want a hammer – you want to build a fence and to do that you need to knock in a nail.

Selling is not about demonstrating every feature and function of your software. It should be about helping a customer to visualise how they could use your software and services or showing how if they had your software, they could solve a problem, achieve a goal or satisfy a need.

Too often sales people focus on 'how' their software or service works and what it consists of – leaving potential customers wondering how they will benefit and uncertain of the results.

If people don't know what problems you will solve for them and the results you will deliver, it is highly unlikely that they will buy from you. However, if you focus on understanding their difficulties and telling them about the outcomes your software can achieve, then your chances of a successful sale are dramatically increased.

Customers will buy from people who they believe to have their best interests at heart. If you have spent the whole meeting informing them about your software or service, they will interpret this as a lack of interest in their business and become resistant to what they feel is just a 'hard sell'. But, if you have talked about how you can help them, then you have built a solid foundation to develop trust and hopefully, an effective and profitable working relationship.

Follow these simple steps when selling your software,
- Understand your customers business
- Understand their business problem
- Then communicate how by using your software or services they will solve their problem.

Achieve Success Selling Naked!

Chapter Two
Improving sales effectiveness

We are all too aware that our economy isn't in the greatest place at this point in time. Over the last few years software sales have become much harder to achieve. During this time I have noticed a growing trend for sales people to reach for their laptop fully loaded with demonstration software and a full set of PowerPoint presentations prepped for a slideshow every time they leave the office.

Now I know this is not going to be used for their homework nor is it designed to improve their product knowledge. This preparation of endless presentations and demonstrations is put together with the belief that in today's economy customers want more and more information about their software in order that they can make that elusive decision to place their purchase order.

Wrong!

Recently I met two sales people enjoying tremendous success. Business was booming yet pricing was virtually a 'non issue' and the response from clients has been staggering – and it's all since they started going into sales calls totally, stark-raving naked! Well, that's how they felt when they were no longer armed with their laptop and corporate brochures. All they had was a notebook and pen!

This attitude encouraged greater interaction and prompted the sales person to find out more about their client's business – its challenges, goals and expectations.

Without a brochure or PowerPoint presentation, you are forced to focus on your client. You cannot direct attention to a software demonstration or other marketing collateral and there is nothing to fall back on – it's just you. This means the entire conversation is client focussed – exactly as it should be, and clients love it as they feel valued and understood.

This particular sales team also reported that they were being asked for advice and even pushed to make specific recommendations for clients and despite this final temptation to pull out a brochure, they instead suggested a second meeting as the next step.

It was during follow-up visits where the sales person then started to introduce proof and evidence of their company to the customer that the significantly larger orders were taken – far bigger contracts than were imagined at the outset.

Chapter Two
Improving sales effectiveness

Selling on Price, you must be joking!

Good sales people have known for a long time that to be successful in sales you need to understand what is important to the buyer - and it's not always price!

In our section "How Customer's select their preferred supplier" we reported that for experienced purchasers price typically came 5th behind the top criteria of

- Levels of support
- Track record
- Software fit; and
- Growth Potential

Selling is an art not a science, it's the art of solving a customer's problems – or meeting their needs, using your software and services. If a customer doesn't have a problem or cannot see a need, then you can't begin to sell - in business-to-business sales, impulse buying simply does not exist.

Selling is about building value for the buyer, not just quoting prices, it's about searching for moments of truth, understanding the real impact of problems and providing solutions that deliver results. That's where I believe many software businesses go wrong – by losing focus of customers' needs and instead, concentrating on their own goals.

We know that sales people are expected to have a smart appearance, a professional and efficient approach and a pleasing manner. Buyers often emphasise that it's more important to demonstrate effective communication – including the ability to question and listen, demonstrate knowledge of the customer's business, their market and their products.

It is a myth that good sales people are considered to be great persuaders. What makes a good sales person is a positive customer perception, this will determine success. Buyers want understandable, relevant presentations and meaningful discussions about their business, their current issues and how a sales person can help them. If they cannot do that, they'll struggle to get past the front door.

Chapter Three
Developing an effective e-Marketing Strategy

Doing business via the Internet is by far the fastest growing sales and marketing medium around – and any commercial organisation that does not put a website at the centre of its sales and marketing efforts can be missing out on vital new customers.

Successful business to business marketing needs a well co-ordinated range of tools driving visitors to their site, for example by using Google AdWords and on-line news releases, but also by 'publicising' the web address at every opportunity – via valuable collateral including newsletters, white papers, surveys, electronic brochures and other promotional materials.

This chapter provides a practical guide to integrating many tools which can dramatically improve the effectiveness of your web presence and drive more visitors to your website converting them to quality leads.

Chapter Three
Developing an effective e-Marketing Strategy

Putting your website at the centre of your sales and marketing!

Doing business via the Internet is by far the fastest growing selling and marketing medium around – and any commercial organisation that does not put a website at the centre of its sales and marketing efforts can be missing out on vital new customers.

These are the thoughts of Software Sales and Marketing Coach, Terry Forsey who believes that all software companies need a website.

"Over the last few years it has become increasingly important that websites are effective, efficient and attractive – in the same way a shop window encourages you to go inside, web pages should make you want to click into the site and find out more," he commented.

"Successful business to business marketing needs a well-coordinated range of tools driving visitors to their site, for example by using Google AdWords and on-line news releases but also by 'publicising' the web address at every opportunity – via valuable collateral including newsletters, white papers, electronic brochures and other promotional materials.

"This means putting the website at the centre of sales and marketing activities, but smaller companies are known for spending time and effort in devising fancy, design visuals using images and illustrations – that although may be technically very advanced – can be unreadable to search engines and not give the potential customer the information they are seeking.

"The wording on web pages is often overlooked and treated very much as an 'after thought'," added Terry. "But it is a critical component in ensuring the site fulfils its 'raison d'être' – stilted text or confused copy will deter sales and alienate buyers. Wording needs to be succinct yet give an accurate description of the service or product on offer whilst highlighting benefits and advantages.

"A good combination of style and content is needed to attract and hold attention – its' not always good enough to do the job yourself – professional input gives professional results, and the investment will be evident to all who visit the site, reflecting the qualities of your organisation."

Chapter Three
Developing an effective e-Marketing Strategy

How to write a great white paper

The use of white papers as a marketing tool has skyrocketed in recent years, not only for selling information technology but also to promote various products and services beyond hardware and software.

White papers can be an effective way to provide the various participants in the sales process with the information they need to make an informed decision. This is especially the case when faced with complex business choices. In such situations, potential buyers need more than just a brochure that simply pitches a product's features and benefits. A well-written marketing or technical white paper (or series of effective white papers) that provides objective, useful information is more likely to be read and influence buying decisions.

Many considerations are involved in writing an effective white paper that aligns with specific marketing and sales initiatives. This article addresses the question of how to write a marketing or technical white paper by focusing on five rules of planning and eight tips for production.

Planning your White Paper

1. Address the Right Topic
Too often, white papers are written in a marketing vacuum, disconnected from real-world sales contexts. And inadvertently, they address topics that neither sales people nor prospective buyers find useful. To close deals, sales people must establish value in the minds of all stakeholders at just the right points in the sales process. Effective white papers can play a critical role in communicating this value.

This is true when customers are considering their options and evaluating technologies. Experience-based knowledge about what real customers are thinking, doing, and asking during the sales process is needed. This is best obtained by involving sales and customer teams early in the white paper definition, scoping, and outlining stages.

2. Define the Type of White Paper
White papers often fail to align with their purpose and role in the sales cycle because the wrong vehicle is chosen for delivering their message. Avoiding this pitfall is simply a matter of proper white paper definition. White papers vary in their structure, and the best type of white paper to accomplish goals and appeal to stakeholders should be carefully considered.

Some of the most common technical white paper types include technology briefings, buyer's guides, planning and implementation guides, application guides, and case studies.

Common business marketing white paper types include business implication discussions, strategy discussions, industry trend overviews, and issues analyses. In some cases, selecting a single white paper type is most suitable, while in others, combining white paper types into a single document may be appropriate.

3. Define the Right Amount of Technical Detail in the White Paper
A white paper that glosses over the details of how an offering helps solve a business problem is little more than a lengthy brochure. By contrast, a document that focuses solely on technical detail without placing the offering in a larger business context fails to make a persuasive case. Effective white papers explain innovative technologies in a compelling way that helps potential customers understand both how and why the offering will benefit them.

4. Ensure White Paper Objectivity
Biased information alienates readers and instils doubt about the paper's validity. Instead of including unsubstantiated claims about the suitability of a product or service, an effective white paper educates the audience about an issue, as well as potential solutions to their problems. To further strengthen the credibility of the business case and to demonstrate the technical prowess of the offering, white paper writers should cite third-party sources, such as analyst research or industry reports, whenever possible.

5. Turn to action
Writing a marketing or technical white paper is not easy. Even with the best white paper plan, a white paper is doomed to failure if the writer lacks the writing skills, technical savvy and marketing experience that these documents require. The task of writing effective white papers requires communication skills that differ significantly from those required for marketing and advertising copy or for technical documents such as user manuals and training materials. If you feel you lack the skills internally to tackle this task yourself then a talented outsourced writer can be of great assistance. These professionals could help defining the scope as well as the content of your white paper.

By incorporating these principles into planning the production of a white paper you can produce effective documents that prove the business and technical validity of a solution and improve chances for sales success.

How to produce your white paper
Writing a white paper is not rocket science, but it is not a walk in the park either. If you are a product marketer, engineer, or sales analyst, and you have planned what you want to write and you are about to start a white paper project, these tips might help.

1. Writing is a Process
No matter how well you write, and no matter how much you love writing, you will not write a good white paper in one draft. It is almost impossible.
Writing is a process. It begins with a first draft and progresses, through many edits and revisions, to a finished piece.

Rather than try to get everything right the first time, focus on writing down everything you know about the subject. Get it out of your head and onto paper - or laptop, desktop, etc...

At this early stage in the process do not concern yourself with structure and logic. There will be plenty of time to make changes during the editing process. Outlines are often helpful. But, don't be afraid to throw one out if it doesn't work for you.

2   Writing should really be Called Editing
Now that your first draft is complete the work begins. Writing a white paper is 2% creative thought and 98% editing.

Expect to revise your paper anything up to 20 times before it is complete. If you want to track your edits try renaming your document each time you complete one revision cycle. Don't try to do all the editing quickly, take time to read and re-read your drafts in different circumstances – over a coffee, in the evening etc.

3   Be Fearless
You may find that you get stuck, during the editing process, because you get emotionally attached to your words. This is not unusual but it is time consuming. When you find that you have spent hours, perhaps days, turning your paper upside down in an attempt to hold onto a cool phrase, a clever metaphor, or a witty joke, then you are stuck!

The answer is to be fearless. Delete anything in your paper that appears too clever, too funny, or extraordinarily literate. You can do it now, or several days from now. But, one way or another, those words will not make it to the final draft. So save yourself some time and be fearless.

As a rule of thumb, never use a metaphor that you have seen used before and avoid humour. It takes a lot of skill to be funny. It is worth remembering that a white paper is an educational piece. Your audience does not expect literary genius. They will be very happy if the writing is clear and concise.

4   Don't Sweat the Small Stuff

Ignore punctuation, spelling, grammar, and usage rules in your first few drafts. There is no sense spending time dotting i's and crossing t's when half of the paper is going to be thrown out and the other half completely rewritten! Keep it Simple and it will be Readable

There are a couple of tricks that you can use to make things more readable. Keep sentences short
Avoid jargon. You can never be certain that the reader and you agree on the meaning of a jargon phrase.

Use simple, straightforward language. Your readers will not be carrying around a dictionary and thesaurus. If they don't understand something you've written they are likely to put your paper down and not pick it up again.

5   Use bullet points
Break it up with clear Paragraph headings.

6   Welcome Other People's Edits
Sending your white paper out for review is a necessary step in the process, but it can be traumatic. Although your paper will be returned with so many comments and corrections that you barely recognise it, remind yourself that each comment is valuable.

You must keep in mind that the edits are not personal. Those red-lines and comments are readers telling you that they love your work, "but wouldn't it be clearer if you said it this way instead."

Don't get upset about the edits. They will make your paper stronger. Better that the marketing assistant corrects a strained metaphor now than to have it staring at you from the pages of a technology journal. It may be the same marketing assistant who worked a miracle and gets your white paper published as a vendor-neutral piece - for the rest of your career.

7   Reading Aloud
Here are a few tricks that can help root out problems that resists all other methods.

Read the paper through - in your mind - in the voice of your favourite TV news presenter. Look closely at any wording that causes you to stumble.
Read your paper aloud. Again, any wording or phrase that causes you to read something twice means there's a problem. Figure out what it is and fix it.

Finally, to flush out some of those truly impossible-to-spot problems change the font and read the paper again. This is a good way to spot echoes - words used twice in the same sentence, or in consecutive sentences.

8   Don't Forget Branding & Positioning
Finally, a tip from that may save not just time, but your paper. Stick with your positioning.

If you fail to take account of the "official" positioning messages when writing you paper you risk stumbling into a region of hell that exists solely for writers of white papers. Sending your paper out for review will prompt conflicting sets of edits from different people, each with their own idea on product positioning messages.

It is not unusual for a sales team to use one set of messages - often tactical and eye-catching - the CEO to use another - strategic and philosophic - and product marketing yet another. Engineering, needless to say, will be the only group that really understands what the product does, and will have their own ideas about what is most important about the product. And customer support, based on actual experience with customers, will have a pretty good feel for what doesn't work, and, hence, what should not be emphasised.

Getting positioning straight is a challenge. If a product positioning document does not already exist you might consider creating one, just to save time later on.

If you think this is a lot of effort, and it can be, remember that your words will take on a life of their own once they leave the confines of your laptop. White papers have a habit of finding their way onto the desks of important people, like the analyst putting together a marketplace overview for some Times 100 company, or the IT Director of that same Top 100 company, as he decides whether to spend a few hundred thousand on your product or your competitors. With this in mind, it is perfectly understandable why so many people would want to influence how you describe your product.

I hope you enjoy these tips and tricks. And I hope they help.

If you embark on a white paper writing project I wish you every success.

Chapter Three
Developing an effective e-Marketing Strategy

Using Surveys to Really Understand Your Customers

Introduction
Who wouldn't want to get inside the minds of their customers and know exactly what they want from your business? What better way to grow your business and look like a hero to your loyal fans. Assuming that sounds good, surveys have got to be a significant part of your market research efforts.

Nothing else gets you direct answers to the specific questions you want answered on subjects as wide-ranging as:

What your customer's like about your business...and what they can't stand;
What you should be thinking about as far as new products or services are concerned;

- Who your customers are - what their segment makeup looks like, what their trends and activities say about them;
- How they'll react to the various business concepts you have racing around your entrepreneurial brain.

And that's just with the first survey you run - subsequent questionnaires can help you dig deeper into specific products or concepts, identify new trends and the information you can mine is gold when it comes to planning future developments in your business.

Including a survey on your website or as part of an email broadcast will allow visitors or recipients to interact with your online marketing. You can offer various types of survey where participants could be anonymous or identifiable.

The survey could just be a bit of fun, on a topical subject to measure the opinions participants, or a valuable way of getting feedback on your products or service from prospects and customers. In addition, the survey results could be used as the basis of a press release, article, newsletter or white paper.

Why use on-line surveys?
How can you improve your business? The obvious answer is to use a customer or market survey. Phone surveys, however, are often irritating. Printed surveys usually have a low response rate, not to mention the expense of printing and mailing. By using an online survey tool, response rates increase and costs are lower. The best part is the ability to view results from each survey-taker and rapidly analyse results.

The analysis and reporting provided by on-line survey tools makes it easy to track trends and view multiple results. On-line surveys are so inexpensive and fast, you'll quickly find other uses for them, such as soliciting feedback on a new service you are considering, a new product you are thinking of developing, and so on.

Chapter Three
Developing an effective e-Marketing Strategy

Getting feedback from your customers through surveys is very inexpensive. You can do it in-house, by emailing or setting up a web form. Or you can use a third party service which makes it very simple and easy to create, implement and analyse customer feedback surveys. I use Constant Contact, but there are many more including Survey Monkey and Vertical Response.

With the customer data you receive, you can further analyse and refine various aspects of your business including;

- Business strategy,
- Customer service guidelines,
- Service or solution packages,
- Pricing and
- Marketing massages.

Careful analysis of this data can help you to increase your business, but most of all, increase sales and overall customer satisfaction. Specifically adopting a strategy of regular surveys will help you achieve some specific marketing objectives, including:

- Identifying trends beyond your day to day view;
- Building a recognised brand;
- Differentiating yourself from competitors;
- Building stronger relationships with customers;
- Identifying weaknesses and determining priorities for action;
- Prioritising and focusing your marketing investment;
- Getting your messages right;
- Driving traffic to your website; and
- Understanding market pressures.

Building a great survey

Customers are more likely to complete a survey when the time to completion is explicitly displayed at the beginning of the process and the purpose of the survey is clearly stated. It is also important to explicitly state what the resulting information will be used for, how will this be published and whether everyone who contributes will receive a copy of this publication.

Successful surveys have a few simple things in common;
- No more than seven questions per survey, (that magic number again!);
- One common topic;
- Short and succinct wording; and
- A multiple-choice format.
- Always examine and analyse the answers. A well-designed survey will reveal trends, patterns and new information all of which will be

valuable components to improving the customer's relationship with your business.
- What are you trying to achieve with your survey?

One of the most effective methods for growing and improving your business is to solicit feedback regarding your products or services directly from your customers.

It is essential to know what you want before crafting the survey what information is being sought. There are many ways the information you gain from customers can be valuable, including:

Gauging overall customer satisfaction
You can see just how satisfied your customers are, and if they aren't, ask them exactly what the problem was and what you can do to fix it. For customers that are satisfied, you can learn more about what they like about your company. Conduct quarterly "client satisfaction" surveys.

Determining customer loyalty
You can test the likelihood that a customer will use your products or services again through their survey answers.

Survey customers and clients on where THEY think you add value (their perspective might be different from yours).

Measuring effectiveness of marketing campaigns
By simply asking the client how they found out about your company, you can see what marketing campaigns are bringing in the sales and which are not, and make adjustments to your marketing efforts accordingly.

Add relevant polls / surveys to your website or newsletters to learn more about your market and start a 2-way conversation.

Identifying interest in new products and services
You can present the customer with sample products and services that you have not yet launched and get their feedback on whether they would be interested in it.

Ask clients or prospects to tell you their biggest frustration or problem relating to your area of expertise. Use this info to develop a white paper based on the most common problems.

Testing new products and services
You can invite current customers to try out a new product or service before you make it available to the public. Then use follow-up surveys to find out how well the product or service is liked, what can be improved and even how to price it.

Chapter Three
Developing an effective e-Marketing Strategy

Include feedback surveys with product literature - use them as testimonial capture device AND to improve future versions of your products or services.

Revealing demographics
By surveying your customers, you can ask them specific questions about who they are and use that demographic information to target your marketing efforts. Survey your market and use the results as the basis of a press release.

Gaining a competitive advantage
You can ask if the customer has tried your competitors' products or services and find out what differences drew the customer to or away from your business and to or from your competitor.

Include a survey in an auto-responder series to automatically capture testimonials.

Send an email to past clients and ask for testimonials and feedback. Structure the survey so respondents provide information on the topics you want.

Developing a better price model
Ask your customers about your prices and use this to understand what they are prepared to pay for certain services or if their buying patterns would change if something were priced differently. You can even get the exact price points for which a customer deems something to be too expensive or too inexpensive to purchase.

Create a short 1 minute feedback survey and include the link in your email signature.

Pre-sales information
If a customer comes to your website, but fails to follow through with their enquiry of purchase, then you can have a one question survey pop up asking why they abandoned the process. This can help you discover problems with your ordering process.

Use surveys to identify prospective customer "hot buttons" so you can craft your sales message in the right way for maximum impact.

Use surveys to capture ideas and strategies from a large number of people to collate into a "master" document.

Conclusion
Surveys help you get inside the minds of your customers and know exactly what they want from your business. Including a survey within your market research will ensure you really understand your customers and your market.

Chapter Three
Developing an effective e-Marketing Strategy

On-line surveys are inexpensive and fast and deliver analysis and reporting to easily track trends and so refine your business strategy, customer service guidelines, packages, pricing and marketing.

Careful analysis of survey data can help you to increase your business, but most of all, increase sales and overall customer satisfaction.

Chapter Three
Developing an effective e-Marketing Strategy

Twelve ways to increase conversions from landing pages

You are unique, there is no one else selling your products and services to your customers with your team. So how can anyone assume that there's a precise formula for success with marketing in general and web marketing in particular.

We all get visitors to our websites. Some remain others depart quickly. If we are lucky we can convert interest into an enquiry.

This paper is about an approach to improving the performance of your website through testing a number of new ideas. Some of these ideas will deliver positive improvements others will not be as successful, for your business.

The basic premise behind this paper is the assumption that you can increase the conversions from Landing Pages. There are three reasons why I say this: Very few sites do the maximum amount possible to optimise effectiveness of each page. Very few people test new approaches.

Unless you are completely satisfied with the performance of your site. You can always improve.

What is a Landing Page?
Let's start with understanding what is meant by a Landing Page. This is the page you send people to from any number of marketing activities. This would include;
E-mails
Pay per Click advertising
Direct mail
Advertising
Etc

Your landing page could be your home page; it could just as easily be another page within your site.

Now before we embark on improving the performance of a Landing Page, let's first ask "what do you want to achieve with your landing page?" What is it that you want a visitor to do when they get to your landing page? It could be a number of things for example
A Sale
A Sign up for a news letter
A sign up for more information
A request to be contacted
Submission of an enquiry

Slicing the Salami
There's no one single thing which will improve the performance of a marketing campaign. There's no magic wand that will have a dramatic effect.

Chapter Three
Developing an effective e-Marketing Strategy

It's like slicing the salami lots of small improvements can achieve a dramatic impact. Therefore the strategy to adopt to achieve improvements is a four step process:

- Experiment
- Test alternatives
- Measure results
- Reach Conclusion

Split Testing
Split testing is a concept that comes from Direct Mail where small changes in a campaign are tested to identify the "better approach".

For example, divide a batch of letters into two random groups and send each group the same mail piece with one specific difference. It may be a different heading; it may be different paper etc.

Then mail to the two groups and measure the response, take action based on the preferable outcome. Continue to refine and improve effectiveness.

The web lends itself to split testing. The key issue is always only change ONE thing. Then re-measure and establish which gets the best results. Continually testing to build quality results.

Again you're looking for small percentage gains each time and combining any number of small gains can result in dramatic improvements with time.

Twelve steps to dramatic improvement in landing page conversion!
So let's focus on these twelve tips. They're not rocket science nor do they require massive financial investment. In fact none of these ideas cost a fortune or even anything in most cases.

Have landing pages that are different to the home page.
This is a relatively simple and straight forward opening idea. Having a landing page that different to the home page allows the landing page to be highly relevant to the visitor. Why is this a big deal? Because the more relevant the landing page the better. People surfing are generally lazy, so do the work for the visitor. Ensure your landing page is specifically focused on the subject they are interested in or attracted by.

Experiment between NO CHOICE & MORE CHOICE
What does this mean well a "No Choice" option restricts the visitor to one specific action? You don't offer navigation, in essence the page is not integrated with the rest of the site.

Whereas with "More Choice", you retain all the normal links to other areas of the site.

Chapter Three
Developing an effective e-Marketing Strategy

Sometimes, depending upon the proposition, offering a page with NO LINKS except sign up / buy option and no other choices can often provide a better conversion than giving the visitor a choice.

Browsing does give you the opportunity to build a relationship with the visitor but increases the likelihood that you might LOSE them from the site all together. Unfortunately there is no certainty so you will need to Test and Measure.

Experiment with different headlines.
What is a headline? It's whatever appears at the top of the page, just like with a newspaper. If you don't have a headline or a banner then the headline is whatever greets them. This could be a picture or a graphic.
People surfing websites make very quick decisions so the purpose of a headline is to keep visitors on your page. So Test and Measure by
- Replacing graphics with words
- Changing headline

Distinguish between above the fold & below the fold.
Think of a large newspaper, this would typically be folded on the news stand. So when you pick it up the first thing you see will be referred to as "Above the fold" – it's what we instantly see on a news stand.

For your website the "above the fold" area is the part of the page a visitor will instantly see without having to scroll down the page. Why is this important? Because a large percent of visitors will make an instant judgement without the effort of scrolling down the page.

So this is telling us we need to test what we include "above the fold" and measure the impact.
Do you have stuff below the fold which if you put it above the fold might help improve conversions; such as contact details, telephone number, an offer etc.
Play around; experiment, test and this will drive improvement.

Positioning – move things around.
Move things around. Move the sign up box from left to right and measure the impact.
Reposition the telephone number or contact details - measure the impact.
Move graphics around – measure the effect. There are NO hard rules.

It's all about experimenting. Play around, test and measure.
The amount of words will have a significant impact. It's not always about more is best. Higher priced items tend to require more words, more content. But if you want a simple action – give me your contact details with a simple message and call to action may work better than a simply "fill the screen" page. And remember to Test and Measure.

Chapter Three
Developing an effective e-Marketing Strategy

Test adding Audio.
Broadband penetration means most businesses, from the smallest, now have a fast internet connection. As a result this means that we are in a multi-media world. This creates an opportunity for communication with potential clients using audio. Test it and see what the impact is. It allows you the opportunity to communicate personally. It may not always work but you will only know if you TEST.

Cautionary note – if speaking and presenting is not something you are good at use a professional or someone you know to do it.
Also test Video. Again you will not know unless you test.

Proof
The internet has provided tremendous opportunity for small businesses to have a huge presence on a world stage. From a back room, a garage or a crofter's cottage in the Outer Hebrides a new business can arise offering considerable competitive advantage.

Unfortunately the Software industry has not always treated its customers well. Clients today need to know that you can really deliver on a promise and not just say you will.

There are three additions to your landing page which build credibility and enhance your proposition:

1.   Testimonials.
Make sure they're on all landing pages. A page specifically for them is fine but incorporate them on all landing pages. While you may look just as credible as the big boys, this proof will set you apart from the field.
So not why combine testimonals with positioning and test the results.

2.   Case Studies.
Sometimes something more that a testimonial is required. This is particularly important where a more complex product or service is concerned.
A case study gives you the opportunity to tell the story of specifically what you have done for a particular customer.
Offer a précis on the landing page with the opportunity to read or download the complete case study.

3.   Use guarantees.
Think about what guarantee you can give. Guarantees help build credibility and reduce the risk for the customer.
Don't be silly with your guarantee be realistic. If you offer a guarantee make sure it's on the landing page, high up, clear and easy to read.
Change your use of pictures and graphics.
There are no hard and fast rules about the use of pictures and graphics on a website. Be careful; if you use pictures ensure that they really add value.
However, words are very important; pictures should not detract from your messages.

Chapter Three
Developing an effective e-Marketing Strategy

Experiment with usage and measure.
Go naked with graphics and see what the impact is.
Move around pictures and see what the effect is?
I'm not saying don't use pictures. If you think that's important experiment and see what the effect is.

Make sure that the words are easy to read.

Telephone number.
If you want people to contact you then make sure the landing page includes your telephone number. This sends a message about availability & credibility. This will tend to increase conversion rate.
Experiment and test. Move it around see what the impact is.

Use the landing page not just to sell stuff but also to build relationships.
Experiment with the position of the sign up box. Play around with the location of where this sits.
- Move it above the fold.
- Move it from left to right or Vice versa.
- Change the wording.
- Have more than one sign up box.
- Measure and test the effects.
- Have multiple landing pages.
- Play around with different pages.
- Perhaps have different landing pages for different key words. Have specific landing pages for email subjects. Reinforce the advertising message with its own landing page etc.

Taking this approach there is no limit the variety and alternatives but you must measure & test. I hope this paper helps you to improve the performance of your website through testing a number of new ideas.

Chapter Three
Developing an effective e-Marketing Strategy

10 Tips to produce an outstanding e-newsletter

Introduction
Recent research identified that around 65 percent of marketers say they plan to increase their use of email newsletters.

It's no secret that offering value to your customers in the form of useful information is one of the best ways to initiate, develop and solidify relationships. But, how do you continue, issue after issue, to make your newsletter stand out in the crowd and keep your readers reading?

What do I write about?
I meet many owner managers of smaller software companies. Very often they say they want to start an E-Newsletter, but what kept them from doing it was that they "had nothing to say." Do you recognise that symptom?
If I asked them to tell me about their best three customers, the issues behind their project, the problems they solved and the impact they had on their business. I bet these same people would have something to say!

In fact I bet you'd have enough information to fill several newsletters!

Running out of material is one of the biggest fears people have - and one of the primary reasons that companies don't launch E-Newsletters in the first place. I have never come across anybody who knew enough about the software industry to start a business in it and who didn't also have a nearly endless supply of content to choose from.

Remember, your customers and others who have an interest in your specialty, don't work in it every day the way you do. The things that are second nature to you, whether it's fixing a corrupt server if you support office networks; how to write programs if you're a software engineer; or how to promote a website on Google if you're a website expert; are all news to those of us on the outside your industry.

These brief, useful nuggets are the things you write about.
The people who are going to read your newsletter have questions. You on the other hand, have answers, opinions, experience, and perspective. When it comes to your industry, you understand what matters and what doesn't, and how all the pieces fit together.

Your challenge in selecting topics therefore, is not having enough to write about. It's identifying which things are the most useful, the most interesting and the most relevant. In short, what topics are most valuable to the reader?

Where to start?
Sit down with a blank piece of paper and write down as many questions as you can think of regarding your business. Write down the things that your customers, prospective customers, colleagues, friends and relatives ask you

every day in relation to your work. When they come to you for an insider's perspective, what is it that they want to know?

You know the sort of questions....
"How do I . . .?"
"Should I . . .?"
"What do you think about . . .?"
"How do I know if . . . ?"
"Is it worth spending money on . . .?
"What would you recommend for . . .?"
"What will happen if . . .?"

All these individual nuggets of information that you work with and think about and pour over every day are the content of your newsletter.

Remember, if you publish your E-Newsletter monthly, you need just 12 good ideas to fill an entire year!

Ten tips to produce outstanding electronic newsletters!
What I'm going to share with you now are the ten practical tips which you can use to make sure that your newsletters stay on track. Here they are:

Make it Useful.
With a business to business newsletter, it's difficult to get any traction with readers if you don't give them some kind of actionable "aha" with every issue you send. Too often, they're inundated by emails, and eager to click the delete button as often as possible.

Your goal therefore, is to give them pause. To make them live in fear that if they delete your newsletter, they will miss some insight that would have made a significant impact on their success.

Useful information rises to the top of the pile, and when your newsletter is on top, you need not worry about how big the pile is.

Make it Engaging.
Great newsletters contain clickable links with a strong call-to action. They might also include compelling links to various pages of your website such as archives of past articles, testimonials, press releases, white papers etc.
The engaging newsletter effectively drives traffic to the website, opening up additional possibilities to convert browsers into enquirers.

Make it Interesting.
I don't know who started the rumour that significant and profitable businesses must also be serious and boring, but it seems to have caught on nonetheless. That's good news for you and me. Because with all the dry as dust E-Newsletters out there, all trying to sound like the front page of the Wall Street Journal, we can make our newsletters shine with little effort.

Chapter Three
Developing an effective e-Marketing Strategy

Personal anecdotes, conversational language and the occasional joke here and there will keep your readers involved long enough for them to hear the "real" information you're trying to give them.

They probably won't read it just because it's interesting, but they certainly won't read it if it's not.

Make it Valuable.
Small pint sized nuggets can be complimented by valuable educational content. White papers can be a very valuable source of information to customers and prospective customers. Just as with this document listen to your customers and prepare materials which interest, educate and, most importantly, is perceived to be of value!

The valuable newsletter can provide a taster to a white paper and drive interested readers to the website to download the complete paper.

Make it Presentable.
Effective newsletters have a clean layout with clear navigation. They use an easy-to-read font and a nice balance of text, graphics and links. Content can be presented both visually, and descriptively. To be engaging they need a warm and casual tone-of-voice that is well suited to their audience, inviting recipients to read further.

Well presented newsletters are opened and read. Readers often come back to read more.

Make it Simple.
An effective newsletter isn't a doctoral thesis; it's not even a case study. It's what I like to call, "a nugget." One insight or tip or concept that your readers can take in, understand, and hopefully remember long enough to put into practice.

If you give too much information (even if it's good), your newsletter could end up being stockpiled, never read, and ultimately deleted because "I'll never get around to reading these old ones anyway".

Give your readers something small enough to understand and remember.

Make it Authentic.
Your E-Newsletter is the voice of your company. It reflects your unique personality and culture, whatever that happens to be.

I've walked into enough companies to know that each of them - even the ones in seemingly straight laced, hard to differentiate industries – have their own language, pace, sense of humour and approach. Don't hide all that in an effort to sound "professional." Marketing is the opposite of fitting in - do yourself a favour and fit out!

Chapter Three
Developing an effective e-Marketing Strategy

Make it Balanced.
Great newsletters include a good mix of promotional and educational material. If you position yourselves as the expert in your field then by sharing advice and providing useful information you are providing a valuable service to readers.

Extending this to encourage readers to take advantage of a service you offer is a natural approach and one which will be well received.

For example: you could include details of ideas and thinking about data storage and protection, perhaps including a relevant white paper and could compliment this with details of a storage audit service which helps identify issues and recommends remedies.

Great newsletters can include promotional items which build on the value of relevant educational content.

Make it Easy - for you.
There's nothing worse than coming up with a great idea for a newsletter content while walking the dog one morning, only to forget what it was when you sit down to write two weeks later.

Keep your list of column ideas in a place you can easily find (I have a task in Outlook called, "Newsletter Ideas"), and every time you think of something interesting for a future issue, put it in there.

Not only does this prevent the "what do I write about" blues, you will be amazed at how quickly the good ideas pile up, now that you have a place to pile them. When it's time to write each month, you simply open the task, look around for the idea that's most compelling, and off you go.

The organised author makes it easy to capture ideas and write compelling content.

The Power of Viral.
Good newsletters often get forwarded to colleagues, business acquaintances and customers. It doesn't hurt to give readers a little nudge by spelling it out, you could explicitly encourage word-of-mouth referrals and newsletter forwarding in their own friendly way. I've seen "Please tell a colleague about our site, and our newsletter. They'll appreciate it, and so will we."

The powerful newsletter solicits referrals and ensures your messages are passed on beyond your present boundaries.

Conclusion
We all know that offering value to your customers in the form of useful information is one of the best ways to initiate, develop and solidify relationships.

Chapter Three
Developing an effective e-Marketing Strategy

Now we can start to see how you can continue, issue after issue, to make your newsletter stand out in the crowd and keep your readers reading!

Identifying the things that are the most useful, the most interesting and the most relevant to your customers will ensure that your e-newsletter is truly outstanding and an excellent tool to grow your reputation and customer relationships.

Chapter Four
Harnessing the power of social media

Each month a staggering 2.7 billion searches are carried out on Google making it the world's number one site. Search engines are great and with appropriate use of keywords and landing pages they can attract customers to your company website. Where search engines fall down is that they have no knowledge of the visitor and can only rely on their search terms to profile them, unlike social media sites.

Facebook is the world's most successful social media site. This site along with others such as Twitter, LinkedIn, and My Space comprise large populations of pre-profiled and pre-segmented potential visitors.

Businesses should be considering the opportunities of using social media to exploit pre-profiled and pre-segmented potential customers as well as building and creating a good reputation.

In particular LinkedIn is great for Business to Business marketing, with over 85 million registered business users. Businesses can create targeted Pay Per Click advertising campaigns that are produced with registered profiles in mind. Facebook works the same way for businesses; however it is more driven towards the Business to Consumer environment.

Twitter on the other hand has grown into a very important business communication tool that enables you to extend your reach. If you have something interesting to post, then post it on Twitter. You can reach even more people when you integrate Twitter with LinkedIn, sending serious business and marketing communications to your connections and followers. Social media has become the new "tool" for effective business marketing and sales.

This chapter provides an introduction to the power of Social media in a business to business world and provides practical guidance in how to make this into a valuable marketing tool to communicate with your customers and potential customers.

Chapter Four
Harnessing the power of social media

The Future of Pay per Click Marketing

What is search engine Pay per Click Advertising?
Pay per Click advertising simply means paying to put a listing or advert for your website at, or near the top of the search engine results. In most cases, it basically means you're paying to get to the top of the search engines.

As an advertiser you bid on keywords which are relevant to your market, you don't actually pay a penny to appear at the top of those results. You only pay when somebody clicks to visit your site. That's why it's called 'Pay per Click.'

How much you pay for each click depends on how much competition there is for the search terms that you want to use, and how high up on the search engine you want to be. Either way, you choose how much to pay – and you can also specify a maximum daily budget. The ability to be able to test your Pay per Click advertising on a small scale is particularly useful for small businesses.

The Google Story
On 23rd October, 2000 Google Inc. announced the immediate availability of AdWords™, a new program enabling any advertiser to purchase the individualised and affordable keyword advertising that appears instantly in Google search results page.

AdWords soon became the vehicle that enabled small companies to compete with the largest businesses on what seemed to be a level playing field. In the early days of Google AdWords you could present an image far beyond your company size. By utilising Pay per Click advertising you could attract many more visitors to your website, rather than relying on the single source of Search Engine Optimisation.

Google is by far the biggest Pay Per Click Company. Others include Yahoo Search Marketing and Microsoft adCenter. Most of your results will come from Google and with 85% of the worldwide search engine market Google is the fastest way to test any new marketing campaign.

Google, to its credit, clearly denotes search listings that are paid placement. In fact, Google AdWords appear in a separate section down the right side of the screen, see Fig 1 below.

Google AdWords allow for nearly instant traffic, which can be turned on and off. Traffic results can be measured, providing information on what is successful, what isn't and what needs to be changed. AdWords that work can be found by running a test campaign and refining the results.

Unlike Search Engine Optimisation, Pay per Click is quick, flexible, and measurable and there are no worries about being banned or blacklisted. You decide how much you want to pay for the position you want to be in for each search term or Keyword(s), Google insists that your site has relevant content

Chapter Four
Harnessing the power of social media

for the search terms you want to target. Because you don't have to wait for a site to be spidered and included in the search engines' indexes you can start getting traffic within a day or so. Unlike Search Engine Optimisation, you don't have to make changes to your sites, so if your site isn't search engine friendly (because of a dynamic content management system, for example, or Flash design), you're not forced to change it.

How does it work?
Advertisers bid on words or phrases, these are called keywords. The more an advertiser is willing to pay the greater the likelihood the advert will appear higher in position in the list of adverts served.

Google, invariably wanting to make the most from advertisers, determines placement based on a combination of click through rate, bid amount and budget.

Of course, in order to maximize revenue and please searchers Google does have guidelines for adverts served and all adverts must receive a minimum percentage click through or they are removed. Targeted click through rates should always exceed 1% and good adverts can achieve well over 10% click through rate.

In fact, Google adverts with a high click through rate get promoted to the top of the page as you can see for my advert in fig 1 above.
Getting Started

First, you write your advert. It needs catchy content comprising a few words of compelling copy to get people to click on your advert. Then you select the keywords that you are going to bid on.

For example, I have chosen to bid on the term 'software marketing' This means that every time somebody searches using these words I want my advert to show up on the pages showing the results of their search.

Next, you need to decide how much you are willing to pay every time somebody clicks on your advert and comes to your website. The more you are willing to pay, the higher your advert will be placed. How much you need to pay to be near the top will depend partly on how competitive your search term is. For example, bidding on the term, 'greenhouse software' will be a lot cheaper than bidding on the term 'Internet marketing', because Internet marketing is a very competitive area.

But here's a word of advice. People can get very obsessed about how much each click is going to cost. Actually, the cost of the click is not what is important. What's important is the business generated by each visitor to your site and whether it's profitable. It can often be worth paying what seems to be a large amount for website visitors, because providing you have selected your keywords properly, these visitors are highly qualified leads and likely to be interested in doing business with you.

Chapter Four
Harnessing the power of social media

Research has shown that people's search terms become more specific with search phrases the further they move along the buying cycle.
The World is changing

For some years many companies myself included have lived in tremendous splendour driving visitors to our website through Google AdWords a seemingly cost effective form of advertising. As with new trends, it wasn't long before everyone started 'jumping on the band wagon' including the larger organisations that would ultimately push up the price of Pay per Click advertising on Google. Today Google AdWords requires a considerable amount more expenditure in order for you to be effective with Click through Rates.

As a regular AdWords user since 2003 I am quite alarmed to see that my own AdWords costs have risen by an amazing 425% from 2003 to 2008, although these increases did drop off a little in 2009.

In a recent survey posted on Twitter, I asked the question "How significant is Google AdWords in your online marketing strategy?" And the responses were as follows;
39% answered Unimportant
20% answered Growing
39% answered Important

From these results, we can see that Google AdWords is still a key tool in online marketing strategies for a significant proportion of the survey participants, however interestingly the exact same proportion of participants claimed that Google AdWords are unimportant.

Consider this situation. We know that Google AdWords enables you to target the specific search term and filter out unwanted terms, but what is to say that a student or a Managing Director of a Times 100 company wouldn't be typing in your selected keyword phrases? In my case if they typed in "software marketing" neither of these people is in my target market and herein lays the problem. I will be paying Google for the privileged of people outside my target market clicking to visit my website.

Fundamentally, search engines have no knowledge of the visitor and only rely on their search terms to profile them.
The future is all about social media!

Now there is a source of potential visitors I would strongly encourage every MD to consider for their business growth. This source is made up of pre-profiled and pre-segmented potential visitors that are registered on social media sites.

By choosing targeted Pay per Click advertising you can select who you advertise to by the Size of Company, Business Sector, Seniority, Geography and other key areas. You may well already be using social networking sites to keep in touch with friends and colleagues and not be aware of the advertising opportunities. My advice to you is to consider a more targeted Pay per Click approach and see what social networking sites have to offer.

At this point, you have heard of social media and inbound marketing. Maybe you have experimented with Twitter and looked at your family's Facebook profiles, and you can see the value for college students who want to make sure they're all at the same bar on Saturday night. But why does any of this matter to you or your business?

Social media and inbound marketing are increasingly important tools for businesses to engage with potential buyers on the web. People have got better and better at ignoring traditional marketing messages and instead go to Google and social networks for answers to their questions. The question for you is: will you be there to answer it?

LinkedIn
LinkedIn is a social network with approaching 60 million users that enables you to make better use of your professional network and help the people you trust in return. It's no secret that LinkedIn is a great place to network professionally, post and find jobs, and answer questions and build thought leadership. It is probably the most obvious way to identify influential individuals at specific businesses. A search for your target business or title on LinkedIn will identify people you may already be connected with, either directly or through your connections. LinkedIn is a great tool to leverage your existing contacts to connect with people and find potential customers online.

Setting up a LinkedIn Profile is simple to do and won't cost you anything. Once your profile is complete, you can start to build your credibility by asking for recommendations from friends, colleagues, partners, and customers. This will communicate your industry experience and add to your credibility.

Find Meaningful Contacts and become active
Connect with people whom you have worked or done business with, or generally people with similar interests or who work in your industry. Invite thought leaders in your industry to connect so that you might establish a relationship with them and, eventually, gain access to their network.

Start with people you know by reaching out to friends, colleagues, relatives and business contacts as this will help you build the first layer of your network.

You can then find people by company. Search under the "Companies" tab so you can start looking for employees that are working in your industry. You can use this method of searching to find the contacts for the types of companies your business is trying to target.

Chapter Four
Harnessing the power of social media

To build a stronger presence you can start asking and answering questions on LinkedIn Answers. In this medium, you will be able to interact and connect with thought leaders, as well as establish yourself as a thought leader in your industry.

Remember to update your status often. Your status appears on your profile and in the LinkedIn Network Updates email to your connections. Thus, others may take notice of what you are working on and decide to connect or click through on links in your status.

You can connect your LinkedIn and Twitter accounts. LinkedIn allows you to connect your Twitter account to your LinkedIn profile via your status. This feature allows you to post a LinkedIn status message to Twitter and to pull a tweet into your LinkedIn status. Enabling this feature will help you leverage both of these networks to build connections on both sites.

LinkedIn for Lead Generation
You can and should use LinkedIn to keep in touch with colleagues and contacts, but LinkedIn's value doesn't end there. It can also be used as a way to generate new leads for your business. The goal is simple: to engage an audience and build a network. You can do this by demonstrating your expertise and thought leadership. Don't sell your services, but feel free to drive people to relevant and valuable content on your website.

You should integrate LinkedIn into your marketing activities. Anytime you do release a new white paper, plan a webinar or attend a trade show or event, invite your audience to network with you or join your group. You can also notify all the members of your group about an upcoming promotion and drive them back to your site to convert them into leads.

Facebook
Facebook is a social utility for connecting people with those around them – friends, family, colleagues, or simply others with similar interests. Facebook started in 2004 as a closed community for college students (requiring users to sign up with a valid university email address) but has since expanded across the world. Facebook allows users to connect and share information in a variety of ways.

Today, Facebook has over 200 million active users and that number continues to grow steadily. It is the third most visited website in the world (behind Google and Yahoo) and the busiest social media site in the world. As early as July 2007, Facebook started calling itself one of the top people/social search engines on the web, though some disagree.

Think your customers aren't on Facebook? There are tens of thousands of regional, work-related, collegiate, and high school networks. More than two thirds of Facebook users are outside of college and the fastest growing demographic is those 35 years and older. While Facebook started off as a community for college students, it has expanded far beyond that and you will

Chapter Four
Harnessing the power of social media

be hard-pressed to find a demographic not yet represented among Facebook's 200 million users.

Facebook ads allow you to promote your business, get more visitors for your business page, and drive more leads for your company. Facebook ads allow you to advertise a website or content you manage on Facebook (like a group, Page, or event). The ad creation and management tools are very similar to the Google AdWords interface.

Next, target the audience for your ad. Facebook allows you to target the reach for your advert by location, gender, age, and interests. As you add filters, Facebook will automatically update the count of people fitting your criteria so you can gauge the size of your target market on Facebook.

You can pay for your adverts in two ways "pay for clicks" and "pay for views." Because the click through rate is notoriously low (less than .1% for most ads), the "pay for clicks" option will offer the best value for the cost. Particularly if you include your company logo as the photo for the ad, you will get a large number of brand impressions to your target audience, and you will only pay for the actual clicks to your Page or website.

Conclusion
There are some fundamental shifts taking place from search engine Pay per Click advertising to targeted Pay per Click advertising within social media sites.

LinkedIn and Facebook offer tremendous potential with current and potential customers undoubtedly being active users. To explore the potential every business should experiment with these sites and identify the opportunities they offer to grow your sales.

Chapter Four
Harnessing the power of social media

The Power of Social Media offers real opportunity for smaller businesses

Each month a staggering 2.7 billion searches are carried out on Google making it the world's number one site. Search engines are great and with appropriate use of keywords and landing pages they can attract customers to your company website. Where search engines fall down is that they have no knowledge of the visitor and can only rely on their search terms to profile them, unlike social media sites.

Facebook is the most successful social media site worldwide. Only today (22nd July 2010) have Facebook announced on the BBC website that their site has reached the 500 million active users milestone. This site along with others such as Twitter, LinkedIn, and My Space comprise large populations of pre-profiled and pre-segmented potential visitors.

It is safe to say that Social Media is a global phenomenon removing all barriers and creating a social 'buzz' amongst its users. Web users are no longer 'content consumers'; instead they are fast becoming 'content producers' with the ability to exchange their content across hundreds of social media sites.

Many businesses are already on the Social Media 'bandwagon' and know how to utilise it as a marketing tool. Businesses should be considering the opportunities of using social media to exploit pre-profiled and pre-segmented potential customers as well as building and creating a good reputation. This is reiterated by David Kirkpatrick, author of The Facebook Effect: The Inside Story of the Company that is Connecting the World, who notes that companies can use the site for advertising and marketing "based on the extremely exact demographic data volunteered by the individual". [http://www.bbc.co.uk/news/world-us-canada-10705923]

In particular LinkedIn is great for Business to Business marketing, with over 70 million registered business users. Businesses can create targeted Pay per Click advertising campaigns that are produced with registered profiles in mind. Clickers arrive direct to your website, exactly where you want them. Facebook works the same way for businesses; however it is more driven towards Business to Consumer marketing.

Twitter on the other hand has grown from announcing what you ate for breakfast into a very important business communication tool that enables you to extend your reach. If you have something interesting to post, whether it is an announcement, an update, a link to another relevant website or article then post it on Twitter. You can reach even more people when you integrate Twitter with LinkedIn, sending serious business and marketing communications to your connections and followers. Social media has become the new "tool" for effective business marketing and sales.

Chapter Four
Harnessing the power of social media

The blog is dead, long live Social Media!

Is blogging dead?
A year ago if I questioned the future of the iconic weblog, people would have thought me mad! But today, in the face of the dramatic explosion of real-time social media services like Twitter and LinkedIn, the future of blogging is far from certain.

It's not just me, many new media pundits are also questioning the future of blogging with obituaries like "Blogging as we know it is dead," being written by Hermione Way, the founder of Newspepper and adding "It's finished."

Are these reports exaggerated? Blogging was invented in the late Nineties as an easy self-publishing tool, a simple way to publish large amounts of static text. The Internet has dramatically evolved over the last ten years from a self-publishing area into a real-time broadcasting platform. The old static blog is indeed dying and is being replaced by Social media.

Today we have Twitter & LinkedIn as the most popular and well accepted B2B social marketing tools. Why is this? It's because these sites have finally empowered the businessman.

They have a voice; they have opinions; they want to share their thoughts, ideas, complaints and experiences. Of course, that's not the only reason people are using Social Media networks, but certainly these are the sort of places people vent.

Many of the old communications which were "blogged" are today being communicated using social media tools. The important thing is that the communication must be brief and relevant otherwise the readers will disappear. In short it must be newsworthy.

As Paul Boutin, from Wired.com writes, "The time it takes to craft sharp, witty blog prose is better spent expressing yourself on Twitter."
News items will still reside on your website and here's a simple process to maximise the effectiveness of News using social media,

- Make sure your LinkedIn account is up to date and maximise your links.
- Add your twitter account to your linked in Profile
- Make sure your e-marketing database is also up to date (This is usually larger than your LinkedIn connections)
- Make sure you are using an e-marketing tool like Constant Contact which also integrates with LinkedIn
- Create an email containing your News/Blog headline & teaser inviting recipients to visit the website article
- Send this to your email database

Chapter Four
Harnessing the power of social media

- The integration of Constant Contact with Twitter will automatically send a Tweet to your followers
- The integration of LinkedIn with Twitter will automatically collect your tweet and post it to your LinkedIn account for all your followers to see.

So now your newsworthy blog has come alive and is integrated with your email database, your twitter followers and your LinkedIn connections immediately receiving your communications through the world of Integrated Social Media.

Search engines are also committed to integrating real-time conversations and fresh content into search results. This presents a huge, immediate opportunity with your content now being tracked as it appears in Constant Contact, Twitter, and LinkedIn and on your website. This approach whilst far reaching does still pull your audience back to your website. Remember, you own the customer, not the Social Media networks.

Chapter Four
Harnessing the power of social media

Ten Twitter tips to help B-2-B Marketers!

Twitter is often one of the most misunderstood and underutilised social media tools. In short Twitter enables businesses to stay connected to their customers and followers and allows them to share information, gather real-time market intelligence and feedback, and build relationships with people who are interested in their business. I think of Twitter as a guidance system to what is interesting, connecting businesses with the right audience at the right time.

Twitter is not a standalone marketing tool but should be integrated with email marketing, newsletter production and other social marketing tools including LinkedIn. Never put your eggs in one basket.

To help you get the most out of Twitter in a B2B environment read my top 10 tips below,

1. You don't have to read EVERY tweet, nor will your followers. The key to successfully using Twitter is being selective.

2. Follow anyone who follows you (and un follow spammers/people you are not interested in).

3. You should pay particular attention to people who retweet your message as this is a good indication they follow what you say and they can be one of your most powerful influencers.

4. Promote other people more than you promote yourself. This keeps your tweets interesting and encourages followers.

5. Retweet the good stuff from others. You will be seen as a source of good information and it helps to generate content.

6. A personalized background means you may be human and encourages tweets.

7. Start thinking in 120 characters; leave 20 characters or more space in each tweet to improve retweeting.

8. Online Tools like Bit.ly let you see stats. Use them.

9. Use Twitter as a personalized communication tool, asking questions can make for very interesting commentary and opinions for blog posts. Twitter is one of the fastest ways of gaining valuable real time feedback.

10. It's okay to tweet your news or blog posts, create interest to lead them into the post. This will increase the impact of your overall marketing activities.

Chapter Four
Harnessing the power of social media

Integrate Twitter with other social platforms, like LinkedIn and invite Twitter followers to Link to you. By creating a fully integrated Social Media strategy your business is more likely to achieve success

Twitter is essentially a platform for building relationships with a broader audience and it's a great way to get real-time feedback from your customers and discover what is being said about your business and the industry you work in. So there is no excuse start Tweeting today, you won't believe how easy it is.

Chapter Four
Harnessing the power of social media

Ten Powerful ways LinkedIn can help you win business

More and more businesses are looking at how Social Media can help them acquire new business. I would like to focus on LinkedIn and explain how incorporating LinkedIn into your overall marketing strategy can help you to win new customers.

LinkedIn is the business oriented social networking site with over 75 million members that will connect you to your trusted contacts and help you exchange knowledge, ideas and opportunities with a broader network of professionals .

Here are ten powerful ways LinkedIn can help you to win new customers,

1. Improve lead generation by gaining an introduction to potential customers, service providers, and subject experts through a mutual, trusted contact.

2. Link to prospects and gain a better insight into their professional background and their company, helping you to show greater understanding and knowledge of their business.

3. Improve your credibility and attract more customers by obtaining recommendations from colleagues and, more importantly Customers.

4. Contact specific people or send general messages to all Linked connections depending on how targeted you want to be.

5. Raise your professional profile by managing the information that's publicly available about you and improve your personal credibility in the eyes of prospects and customers.

6. Increase the profile of your company by building a company page and encourage people to follow the company as well as linking to you personally.

7. Integrate your LinkedIn account with Twitter and all your tweets will automatically be notified to your connections.

8. Advertise to highly targeted, pre-profiled groups of business professionals worldwide.

9. Follow different companies and get notification about their news and updates so you are aware when to make specific contact and who to target.

80

Chapter Four
Harnessing the power of social media

10. Post and distribute job listings to find the best talent for your company

Being the world's largest professional social network, LinkedIn is a resource that shouldn't be ignored. Adding LinkedIn to your marketing strategy can help your business win new customers and build your professional reputation by connecting you to sales leads and ideal business partners.

Chapter Four
Harnessing the power of social media

The new social PR Platform

Small Businesses need a superior alternative to email for exchanging information for publication. Sites such as PitchEngine are the new social PR platforms. As we see the Word Document Press Release disappear, the start of a Social Media PR revolution is on the horizon.

Unlike traditional wire services, PitchEngine enables you to create and share your own content, including images, videos and attachments. This is aimed not just at journalists, but also to bloggers, followers and influencers too. PitchEngine's excellent SEO capabilities enable strong brand building through exceptional indexing in major search engines.

"The days of creating and pushing one press release are over. These are the days of reaching diversified and equally pivotal communities when, where, and how they choose to be reached", reports Brian Solis, author, speaker and PitchEngine advisor.

PitchEngine is an excellent tool for anyone wanting to become engaged in social media. Originally set up in the Rural Mountains of Wyoming, PitchEngine is now a global success. Having only promoted themselves through social media, they now serve over 100,000 businesses worldwide. These businesses understand Social Media is all about the conversation than the "push" of traditional marketing and PR tactics.

With PitchEngine, you create and share a Pitch™, a social media version of the press release. Unlike the traditional press release, your Pitch™ can incorporate embedded video, images, PowerPoint and more into a hosted "microsite" that can easily be shared via the social web using apps such as Facebook, Twitter and LinkedIn.

The Pitch™ engages readers, by its conversational style that blends elements of traditional PR with more progressive social methods. These readers are not just from the media, but investors and consumers alike.

As PitchEngine enables us to say 'Goodbye' to our traditional Word Document PR, it also eliminates the need for a press kit.

Other features and services that PitchEngine offers are;

Monitor and Track the Conversation, so you know how many people viewed your PR content and how it plays out across different mediums.

PitchEngine offers an attractive 'basic' plan, free for the first 30 days, then limited to one published pitch per 30 day period.

For those of you with greater usage there a monthly subscription-based service with no long-term commitment as long as you're a customer your pitch will remain live and indexed.

Chapter Four
Harnessing the power of social media

Small to medium software businesses should be taking advantage of social media PR platforms in order to 'spread the word' across a variety of reader groups. Take this opportunity to improve your brand presence and reach a wider audience.

Chapter Five
Executive support to tackle real business issues

New skills are not acquired in the classroom. Tiger Woods doesn't learn how to hit the ball 300 yards by studying text books. Wayne Rooney is not in the habit of sitting at a desk when developing on his natural ability to dart round defenders and score goals from 25 yards. No! they learn by practical exercise.

The same principle applies to business growth - there comes a time when you just have to leave the theory behind. Just as Tiger and Wayne work with professional coaches, so a great software business is developed through coaching.

This chapter demonstrates some of the ways a professional business coach can help you with practical experience and hands on assistance.

Chapter Five
Executive support to tackle real business issues

Protect your customer base from your competition

Many software companies are differentiated NOT by their products or their solutions but by their people and the service they deliver.

It's not just their people that make the difference, it is what they do and how well they do it that really counts.

The behaviour of their people is at least fifty percent of the service they deliver, so what exactly are the key behaviours which make a business truly customer centric? In tough economic times it is crucial that you are confident that your customer base is safe.

Within this paper we look at eight critical criteria that can help deliver a customer centric service, one which will help protect your customers from competitive threats!

Take a look at these criteria below and ask yourself the question: "On how many would my customers give me (or my company) eight out of ten?" If your answer is "all of them", then there are two explanations for your answer. The first is that you are the God of service (which is unlikely) and very successful to boot; the second (and much more likely) is that you are kidding yourself.

The first step in self-improvement is to admit your weaknesses. So be honest. Look at each of the eight and be objective and non-defensive. Talk to your colleagues about it and, if you really want to know the truth, ask your customers!

1.   Appreciation

Customers like to feel valued.
Regardless of whatever else you have to do, customers should always be your number one priority. They need to feel valued, after it is true that "customers pay your wages".

Accountants or managing directors don't create wages; customers do. You can have the most persuasive sales team, the most creative marketing department, the most numerate accountants, the most brilliant technicians or the most strategically-gifted Directors; if enough customers decide that they would rather buy from one of your competitors rather than you, none of it is worth a carrot.

The other part of appreciation is courtesy.
Courtesy involves using people's names. It was Dale Carnegies who once wrote, "The sweetest sound in the whole world is the sound of your own name."

Courtesy includes expressions like 'please' and 'thank you' but is much more. It includes little phrases like "No problem" or "I'll be glad to do that." I am always struck by the difference between the manner of the average American telephone operator and the average UK one. They are doing a repetitive job that requires speed; unfortunately many operators are hired for their efficiency and no-nonsense attitude. Well, they might be efficient, but they can also be abrupt. American operators, on the other hand, will usually say "Sure, no problem" or "I'll be glad to do that." It's only a small thing, but it's important.

2.   Accessibility

Can your customers access your service easily?

This is all about availability, i.e. Can they get hold of you when they want to (not when you want them to)? So many companies seem to delight in making it difficult to get hold of anyone.

The telephone is a minefield for customer service, and far more people will have bad telephone-related tales than good ones. Let's look at a few of the things that can go wrong with the telephone.

Speed of response

"Answering the telephone in three rings" is a cliché and something which companies often see as a relatively easy 'quick fix,' but having said that, it is important. Answering the telephone quickly is sign of appreciation; it shows you value the customer and what they have to say.

Most of us might wait in a queue for ten minutes before becoming annoyed but wouldn't dream of doing the same thing on the telephone. In a queue, you know what's happening. One of the most psychological needs a person has is to feel in control of what is going on. In a queue, you can see what is happening and constantly re-evaluate how long things are going to take. On the telephone you don't know what's going on. If it is just ringing and ringing, you just don't know!

That's why people like systems that tell them "you are fourth in the queue ..." because it's the equivalent of being able to see how fast a queue is moving. So much better to have a real person answering quickly!

IVR Systems

While IVR (interactive voice response) systems are a very cost-effective way of dealing with telephone calls, the 'press 1 for this, 2 for that' approach is universally hated by customers. A bad experience may well lead to the customer hanging up. You have to decide what you are trying to do: reduce costs or keep customers? Call centres may be focused on speed and cost-effectiveness above all else, and the result is service that is robotic, mechanical and soulless.

Small software companies can differentiate themselves with a personal service so the customer feels that they're not just a number and that the operator's main objective is to get rid of them as quickly as possible.

Chapter Five
Executive support to tackle real business issues

Operators are 100% effective at recognising a stressed caller and responding accordingly. "John, we've got Mike on line one. He sounds pretty tense!"

Opening hours
Whatever your opening hours, (9am to 5am or 24/7), it's vitally important that everyone in the team is ready to deliver 100% service from the first minute to the last. Arriving at work at 9am reading emails, having a coffee and taking calls from 9:20am, is in reality, ignoring customers for 20 minutes!

3. Reliability

Reliability is that number one thing that affects customers' perceptions of the service they are receiving. It can be defined as "Do you do what you say you are going to do?" and it covers not only big things like delivery schedules, but also small things like returning telephone messages and replying to emails.

Never make a promise unless you are 99% certain you can keep it.
Often the temptation is to agree with customers and promise to do something when you know it will not happen, just to shut them up! By doing this not only are you digging a hole for yourself, you are also tampering with possibly the most important behaviour of them all.

Keep the customer informed
Promises often involve a deadline. If you can't make that deadline for any reason, pick up the telephone and tell the customer. They might not be happy, but they will be a lot happier than if they are left in the dark. Particularly if the first time they know a deadline will not be hit is when it has come and gone.

So although they might not say it at the time, if you tell customers when you cannot meet a deadline, most of them will at least think "thanks for letting me know". You can even turn a negative into a positive by keeping the customer informed.

4. Speed
Can you think of anything (apart from traffic) that is slower nowadays than it used to be? We live in a society increasingly characterised by the search for instant gratification. Everything is now, NOW, NOW! Today we expect everything to be open twenty-four hours a day. If we want to do our banking at 3am, we expect to be able to do it via the internet. We want everything instantly and expect the same of our software suppliers.

Today, customers expect an email response in 2 hours or want an "out of office" message.

Unfortunately many software companies have not caught up with this fact, and still act as if it was the 1970s. While their customers' expectations have changed, their processes haven't and the danger is that they begin to look like dinosaurs in this "faster than the speed of light" age.

Chapter Five
Executive support to tackle real business issues

Changing processes
Many processes have unnecessary and redundant steps, which are only there for 'belt and braces' purposes. Have a look at your processes (all of them) and ask yourself the questions: what would happen if I took this step out of the process? Would it be the end of the world? Would the sky fall in? Or would things simply be a bit quicker?

5. Confidence

Positive language
You can probably think of a number of people you know that when you ask them to do something, can instantly come up with half a dozen reasons why it can't be done.

You can no doubt also think of people (but the list will probably be shorter) who when asked the same question will have the same problems, but will find a way to help. Why? Because they are 'can-do' people and the former are 'can't-do people'. It does not need the brains of Einstein to realise that customers prefer "can do people".

Instead of being told how expensive, difficult, time-consuming, inconvenient or tricky their request is, they want a response along the lines of "no problem" or "leave it to me or consider it done".

Guarantees
Another way to instil confidence in customers is to have guarantees. As all suppliers claim to give great service, customers subconsciously discount these claims by about 50%, thinking "well, you would say that, wouldn't you; you're trying to sell me something." Some suppliers, however, are confident enough about their service to be able to give guarantees, which in turn generates confidence in their customers.

A type of guarantee tells the customer what to expect in specific, quantifiable terms. You can incorporate this into a customer service charter that tells the customer what he/she can expect in qualified terms. What is the company's overall approach to service issues? What type of reaction can he/she expect when there is a problem?

Such guarantees make the customer think, "They must be efficient and good at what they do, because they couldn't give that kind of guarantee if they weren't." in other words, it fills them with confidence.

Are there any guarantees that you could give? If you can identify an aspect of your service at which you excel, why not attach a guarantee to it? For example, if your delivery reliability is 99%, you can offer a 10% reduction on any delivery that was late. It won't cost much and will probably be offset by the extra business it generates.

Chapter Five
Executive support to tackle real business issues

6. Empathy

The average software company is, unfortunately, very internally-focused, its processes are often there for its own convenience and the customer is expected to 'like it or lump it' and fall into line. Most companies do not look at things from the customer's points of view; they expect the customer to look at things from theirs.

How many times have you heard the dreaded words, "I'm sorry sir/madam, you don't understand our system ..."? This phrase should be banned from the English language, because as soon as you hear it, you just know you are about to be told why what you want is impossible.

Rather try to differentiate yourself from the larger, less customer centric businesses. Commit, from the Managing Director downwards, to changing your approach and communication to really empathise with your customers.

7. Flexibility

To show empathy, of course, you need flexibility. Too many people cling to rules and procedures because they give structure and meaning to their lives. Such people are life's 'jobsworths'.

All companies need rules; without them you'd have chaos. But with exceptions of health & safety, rules are there for 95% of the time. For the remaining 5% the rules don't apply. Why not? Because common sense tells you so.

8. Helpfulness

Let me start by asking you a question. If you called a technical support centre and asked for help, and were answered with "Certainly, what can I do for you?" would you be impressed?

Think about this for a second, because if you answered "yes" I don't believe you. Are you saying that you expected the reply, "Get lost, can't you see I'm busy?"? Of course not. If you ask for help, you expect to receive it and you're generally not impressed when you get it. The point is that offering help when a customer asks you for it isn't impressive. It's what the customer expects.

Companies that are famous for service, train their employees to give help that is above and beyond anything the customer expects, and to offer it before the customer has asked or in circumstances where the customer didn't even think help was possible.

Conclusion
So you've considered how your customers would rate you on these eight critical behaviours that can help deliver a customer centric service. How high

Chapter Five
Executive support to tackle real business issues

do you rate? Where should you concentrate your efforts to achieve real improvements in the service your company delivers to your customers?

Improving your service gives you an outstanding opportunity to distinguish your company and really differentiate your service so that you will be able to outperform other, less effective, competitors. Now that's a goal worth achieving.

Chapter Five
Executive support to tackle real business issues

Six make or break factors for entrepreneurial success.

Being a successful entrepreneur is a bit like racing in the Grand National. There are many starters, you'll meet unpredictable fences and the 'going' and weather conditions affect each runner differently. Once the race starts, there are soon lots of fallers, some run out of the race and others lack stamina and give up. You end up with very few finishers who complete the course.

This is a good analogy for the business world today. Many small owner managed businesses are finding the going tough. Some may even be on the edge of giving up!

Yet if you read the press or watch the TV you will see that there are many winners, many successes of the business world - the multi-millionaires. The reason is all about how these guys deal with the race and the obstacles they have to tackle.

This paper is all about the six big obstacles you will have to successfully navigate. They are the crucial fences you will inevitably face. How you tackle them will determine how you fare in the race to win in your business. Smart entrepreneurs will be aware of them from the start and plan how they will overcome each one before they have to face them in their race.

Obstacle 1 - Being hesitant about selling.
This is the big one. Most business owners I meet are very reluctant sales people. Why? Because they went into business because they were technically very competent. I often hear them say "Why work for someone else when I can work for myself". These budding entrepreneurs are prepared to put in the hours and effort it takes.

Sadly the quality of their passion and their core technical abilities will mean absolutely nothing if they can't sell what they have and do so really effectively and passionately.

Being hesitant about selling, having concerns like "I'm not a sales person"; "I don't want to be pushy" is the biggest killer for a lot of new business. To be successful you, as the owner of the business, must now become a professional sales person. So your ability to really create the success you deserve will depend on your willingness to become a great sales person.

You will realise that much of what you hear about sales people being sharp or dodgy is just nonsense. Sure there are some unscrupulous people out there but to be successful you will have to embrace the selling process; you don't have to be pushy you have to be able to communicate with certainty and passion that you can deliver something of real value to your customers and show that you will deliver.

Chapter Five
Executive support to tackle real business issues

So to have a successful business without a successful sales person is virtually impossible.

You owe it to yourself and your current and potential customers to be really good at selling. Why? Well if you have something valuable, which can really make a difference to them you owe it to potential customers to communicate this message effectively and passionately to help them to help their businesses.

The starting point is your mindset and from this comes the motivation to acquire the selling skills you will need to be successful. The mindset to become a professional sales person will transform your business; the mind set is

"I am a professional sales person";
"I owe it to my potential customers to clearly communicate the value and benefit of what I can do for them"; and
"I can then confidently ask them for their business".

It is this mindset that provides the motivation to seek out coaching for your sales skills and commit the time needed to perfect these skills.

Selling is the vehicle that will make your business successful. So be proud of your business and sell with pride.

Obstacle 2 - Don't allow enough time!
When you have a sales and marketing operation established in your business you can make big changes very rapidly. Unfortunately, in the early days of establishing a new sales and marketing process the route to market will have lag time to achieve results.

When considering what is possible from your sales and marketing activities, be conservative, extend your timescales to give you the space and capacity to be successful.

I'm not saying work slowly; I'm not saying don't act with urgency and enthusiasm but when planning a marketing campaign or a sales activity don't assume that your enthusiasm will deliver instant results. Build time contingency into your planning so if the first customers buy slower or buy less that you expect then you're not dead and buried. You can deal with these challenges.

Everything doesn't always go to plan. Marketing is an imprecise science and trialling and testing will allow you to get it right BUT you will inevitably get a few things wrong along the way. So allow time for this experimentation and rework.

When establishing a sales and marketing process factor lag-time into your planning to ensure the space to succeed.

Chapter Five
Executive support to tackle real business issues

Obstacle 3 - Don't charge enough.
Too many new businesses stumble and fall at the pricing hurdle. As a business owner and entrepreneur, you must be personally rewarded for your endeavours and generate sufficient income to pay for all staff, overheads and supplier costs.

Too often pricing is the difference between success and failure for the smaller business. It's a myth that everyone buys on price. Only a small proportion of businesses buy exclusively on price.

When a product or service reaches commodity status, sales are predominantly made on price. It is, though, rare for new entrants to enter a commodity market in software.

Before you start to consider your pricing model you will need to be clear why someone will buy from you. Can you clearly state what value you bring to potential clients? What is it that you can do for them that they will value?

Now your customers will always try to tell you that price is important but do you really think if you are seeking a mutually beneficial long term relationship that they would be happy to see you price yourself out of business?

Printing is often regarded as the most competitive market. If you've ever gone looking for a good printing supplier you're aware how time consuming and difficult a task that can be. And even when you've selected your preferred supplier the problems and challenges can continue. If you've ever been there would you be prepared to pay 10-15% more for a reliable dependable and quality service? Would you pay more for a hassle free supplier who comes up trumps time after time?

Not only that, but once you are happy with your supplier do you always seek competitive quotations? Or will you allow your supplier to work their prices up to protect their margins?

So can you identify what it is about your products or service that customers' will value. This will allow you to price to reflect the quality and value of what you offer? If you can, then you will not be forced to be the cheapest!

Large companies will continuously test their pricing, reworking ideas, test price rises, new price configurations etc.

So from this perhaps you can conclude that today you may be sitting on untapped additional profits which, if you test your pricing model and rework your prices in specific areas, you may well be able to charge more for your products and services.

Chapter Five
Executive support to tackle real business issues

Further more if you really get your marketing machine flying and you can positively influence your customer's perception of you and your value then the resistance to higher prices reduces accordingly.

As a goal in the next six months look at all areas of your business and determine one area where you can increase prices by at least 10%.

Obstacle 4 - Don't take action.
All the information in this paper has no value until you take action. Your ability to take large amounts of action will determine your level of success. The top 1% of highly successful entrepreneurs are virtually "addicted" to taking action. They are always implementing.

If you can adopt this habit, this will start to transform your business. Often when someone has a brainwave or reads about something interesting or hears of a good idea they park it, put it on a list or plan to come back to it. This is not what the great entrepreneurs do; they become conditioned to take action today.

There's no shortage of knowledge available to business owners, there are books, CDs, DVDs, consultants, business clubs etc. That's not the issue; it's what you do with the one or two ideas which really resonate with your business. The issue is will you get out there and do something?

The real reasons why we don't take action are often
- Lack of time - you need to prioritise what you're doing to give you space to take action and;
- Fear of failure – we have been conditioned to fear failure and this prevents us from taking action.

You can soon get to the point where you want to do things even if they're not successful. They become learning points and from them you can discover great lessons.

Great entrepreneurs do many things which do not work. Successful people DO make mistakes. They often make many mistakes as they take lots of action. I'm not saying take unnecessary risks but get obsessive about transforming ideas into action.

Make taking action an absolute key part of your business life and use the mistakes to learn more about yourself, your business and your market.

Obstacle 5 - Always look for perfection.
Too often we want everything perfect before we take action. The problem is that nothing happens. It may be necessary to achieve 100% perfection in a recording studio. For the other 99% of us it is not necessary to be perfect before we take action!

Chapter Five
Executive support to tackle real business issues

We have not been conditioned to be like this, particularly if we have an academic background, the culture is to take the time to get it right. Entrepreneurs need to take actions. If there is something not quite right at the outset well they'll correct it later! This might seem counter intuitive, it may sound irresponsible but it's true.

Too often the "not quite right yet" argument is used to prevent action. The result is often a never ending chase after a receding target.

Examples of this are;

- A website, I say launch it when it's better than the current version, and then draw up a priority list of improvements.
- New software product launches, I say when it's almost ready, release it as a Beta and get the market place to determine the priority fixes.
- Mail shots or flyers, I say take them to the pub or to some friends and get their feedback. You will notice that they never read every word and will have a few high level observations. Act only on these issues.

Very often a less than highly polished item can often have a positive effect.

Unless there are specific reasons don't get obsessive about perfection. Instead replace it with action!

Obstacle 6 - Don't think big!
If you're reading this you are obviously seeking some form of personal or business improvement. Sadly, today too many business owners are not beginning to touch their real potential.

If you sell a product or services that people really want and you are willing to really go for it then you will have a dramatic advantage. Furthermore, if you're reading this you're probably thinking bigger than the silent 80% majority. That majority, more often than not, will include your competitors!

If you're interested in doing something to improve your business then start to think big! How many people around you are encouraging you to think big? Typically, it would be very few.

You want to make extraordinary success. How many people around you are seeking the same? Typically, you may find them not too encouraging.

So start to mix with successful people, read about them, talk to them. Thinking big is throwing away your inhibitions. You will not be successful if your mind is not open to it.

Chapter Five
Executive support to tackle real business issues

Set your targets high, think big and seek out people who have been successful and who will encourage you to do the same.

Conclusion

So you are now armed with an understanding to tackle the six big challenges that you will inevitably face in your entrepreneur's race. To summarise these are;

- Selling is the vehicle that will make your business successful. So be proud of your business and sell with pride.

- When establishing a sales and marketing process, factor lag-time into your planning to ensure the space to succeed.

- As a goal in the next six months look at all areas of your business and determine one area where you can increase prices by at least 10%.

- Make taking action an absolute key part of your business life and use the mistakes to learn more about yourself, your business and your market.

- Unless there are specific reasons don't get obsessive about perfection. Instead replace it with action!

- Set your targets high, think big and seek out people who have been successful and who will encourage you to do the same.

With this awareness you can now start to plan how you can overcome each one before you have to face them in your race.

Chapter Five
Executive support to tackle real business issues

The Value of Non-executive Directors in helping Software Companies through this recession.

Most people have heard the term Non-Executive Director often without actually knowing what they are, much less what they can potentially do for a small and growing software business to help them weather the storm of the recession.

But those who are in on the Non-Executive secret know that they can add knowledge, contacts and general 'been there, done that' wisdom to a company's board. All of which cannot fail to be of value to a company whatever its size and this is particularly important as businesses have to chart the uncertain and unfamiliar waters of a recession.

Many businesses have recognised the potential of Non-Executive Directors. Research indicates that companies with one or more effective Non-Executive Directors typically perform better financially than those without.

What is a Non-Executive Director?
A Non-Executive Director sits on the board of a company alongside the Executive Directors. They act as an independent voice on every important decision. He or she will not work full time, though, and won't be concerned with all day to day issues.

They will have a good understanding of the running of the company. This means knowing what each person does and being familiar with monthly sales figures and accounts. This allows them to make informed decisions in the interests of the company.

There is a difference between the role of a Non-Executive Director in a larger company and one in a smaller one. In larger businesses, most of their time will be spent in board meetings. Smaller software companies often need someone who is willing to roll up their sleeves and get involved in specific issues on the days they are in the office.

What can a Non-Executive Director contribute to the Board?
A Non-Executive Director working alongside the Executive Directors of a growing software company can help in many very practical ways;

- Providing objective and independent assessments.
- Bringing management skills to complement the existing team.
- Being a sounding board for the company's executives.
- Coaching and mentoring fellow Directors;
- Providing sector knowledge and contacts.
- Providing an external view of the business, the market they operate in and the opportunity it presents;

Chapter Five
Executive support to tackle real business issues

- Representing the Customer within the Board and taking a customer centric view in discussions and decision making;
- Questioning and challenging new ideas and existing business practices
- Supporting decision making - challenging views, exploring alternatives, prioritising alternatives and helping reach better, more timely, decisions;
- Helping bring clarity and focus to the business strategy;
- Bring experience and calmness to the management of crisis;
  And in these challenging times, bring experience of coping with an economic downturn and helping to develop survival strategies.

Early stage businesses often operate in an environment with lots of unknowns. While Non-Executive Directors do not carry a magic wand, they do bring experience to draw upon to tackle new situations. They can provide a process to think through issues and support to ease significant decisions.

For many growing software companies, selecting a Non-Executive Director with a strong Sales and Marketing background can often provide balance to an otherwise technically focused Board. As the company grows its sales and marketing resources, the experience of the Non-Executive Director can ensure the right people are selected.

What qualities should they have?
If the company is an especially young one, the Non-Executive Director is often expected to provide a few grey hairs to the board. Not necessarily age wise - although this is likely if the staff are as young as their business - but in terms of relevant business experience.

He or she should have a proven business background and sound business judgment and, in reality, they are likely to have significant experience of the software sector.

For a start-up company, Non-Executive Directors will often be entrepreneurs themselves - because this stage of a business is more within their direct field of experience. There will be less of a fixed routine and these are the kinds of people who will respond well to this.

Do I need a Non-Executive Director?
The appointment of Non-Executive Directors is not "cosmetic window dressing". Non-Executives should be an independent sounding board and bring an input to strategic thinking for the further development of the business. Directors clearly know their business; Non-Executive Directors should positively contribute to the future development of this business.

The right Non-Executive Directors will add credibility to the company's presentation to bankers and potential investors.

Chapter Five
Executive support to tackle real business issues

If you are raising investment funding, the investors will certainly wish to have "their" Non-Executive Director on the Board. Unfortunately, they may not add much independent value, since they consider the interests of the private investor ahead of yours. To balance this situation, having your own Non-Executive Director would definitely be an advantage.

Your Non-Executive Director will help you weather the storm of recession, adding knowledge, contacts and general 'been there, done that' wisdom to a company's board. .

Businesses with one or more effective Non-Executive Directors typically perform better financially than those without.

When choosing your Non-Executive Director, pick someone with relevant experience and whose opinions you respect. If you select the right person, your Non-Executive Director can be a valuable asset to your company and ensure a profitable future.

Chapter Five
Executive support to tackle real business issues

Experience is crucial for business success!

There are hundreds of sources of small business advice out there to choose from. Smaller Software businesses must be sure that when looking for help and assistance in sales and marketing that time is taken to consider the following crucial points;

Put your business in safe hands. As an owner and manager of a small software business you have had to work hard to get to where you are today. When looking for advice and guidance look for someone who has walked your walk. Look for a skilled and mature expert with over thirty years in the software industry and who knows the small business market inside out.

WARNING Avoid generalists and academics too much theory can cause you headaches.

Whilst you're looking for experience also look for energy and, drive. Look for a consultant who will work for you enthusiastically to help improve your sales and marketing.

If a consultant only works for owners of small software companies, you get to share in what works for their other clients and, equally important, what doesn't work.

Make sure they're cost effective and not just cheap! If a consultant understands the software industry and small businesses they will not need three or four days to familiarise themselves with your situation. They should be able to provide a thorough brief to scope their work and they should be able to spread the cost of improvement programmes over several months, you can start to experience the benefits of these services without it hurting your pocket!

Look for a consultant who offers you personal attention. Make sure you are not "passed off" to a junior. Equally important be sure they're not too busy to return your calls and emails promptly. If the consultant is unavailable can you be sure to speak to a person and not an answer phone.

Don't just take their word for it; see what their clients have to say. Ask for testimonials and case studies, call and speak to their clients ...

Put them to the test; ask for a "free-no-obligation" consultation during which you can decide if they are the right person to help your business.

Chapter Five
Executive support to tackle real business issues

Preparing your business for peak season

It is widely acknowledged that the autumn months of September, October and November are peak business months for UK companies; it is not surprising therefore that companies choose this time of year to launch new products.
As schools return in September, staff return from summer breaks invigorated and ready to throw themselves into a new project or challenge. This is great, but it is now that businesses should already by thinking about ways in which they can maximise their sales and marketing potential during this fast approaching peak season.

Do not leave the planning and organising to the last minute, with only eight weeks to go until September you have a lot to do to prepare your Sales and Marketing activity for the autumn.

Marketing campaigns need to be carefully planned. Make sure you know who you are targeting, how you are going to reach them and what resources you have to do that. While things are a little quieter during the summer make sure that all of your resources are up to date including website content, sales presentations, brochures and other marketing collateral.

Remember, good sales initiatives need well thought out collateral.

Chapter Five
Executive support to tackle real business issues

Working collaboratively to achieve success

Following the General Election the nation is pinning its hopes on the Conservatives and the Liberal Democrats being able to work collaboratively to effectively and successfully run the country.

Being able to develop strong working partnerships with colleagues, peers and external organisations isn't always easy, but it is critical if you want to achieve success.

Working collaboratively is something all businesses have to do on a regular basis. It can bring many business benefits such as sharing ideas, resources and costs, speed of delivery etc. Not all businesses however find the transition to collaborative working very easy.

I would like to outline my thoughts for successful partnerships, whether they are with external partners or internal departments.

Collaborative working is often considered when difficult projects need to be tackled and neither party can tackle them alone, as the old saying goes 'A problem shared is a problem halved'. Before embarking on any collaborative project, a small business should consider the following,

Agree on the outcome of the collaboration– this is the most important key to a successful collaboration. Make sure that all parties are very clear in what they want to achieve from working together, and continually revisit this to keep the collaboration on track.

Be open to new ideas and maintain an open mind – everyone needs to have their ideas heard, prepare to listen well to all parties and keep an open mind before narrowing down the focus.

Be clear about who 'we' is – when launching a collaborative venture, make sure it is clear that you know who is undertaking each part of the project.

Be sure to understand your potential collaborator– How informed are you about the organisation that you wish to collaborate with? In order to collaborate successfully you must know enough about the organisations and individuals that you will be working with.

Be clear what's in it for both parties - for a collaboration to work the outcome for each party needs to be clearly articulated and be seen to be fair and equitable. If this cannot be established early in the relationship a collaborative partnership is unlikely to fly.

Chapter Five
Executive support to tackle real business issues

Invest in building strong relationships– a successful collaborative working partnership is built on openness, trust, honesty and respect. These relationships need to be carefully built.

Be sure to communicate well – Good communication of all types and at all levels is the key to achieving a strong working collaboration. Establishing a framework for regular formal and informal communication will reap great rewards.

Have a reflective approach– Be prepared to try things out, but always reflect and evaluate, making adjustments and if it is not working, then don't do it.

Capture the energy and enthusiasm– Collaborative working results in a larger pool of ideas and input that often results in a 'can do' attitude. If a decision feels right and everyone agrees then just go for it. It can lead onto greater things.

While the country waits with baited breath to see how successful our newly formed coalition government will be, you should start to consider (if you haven't already) how collaborative working could bring success in your business. Before you decide to embark in a working collaboration, be sure to consider the pointers outlined above – they will help you to set up a successful partnership.

Chapter Five
Executive support to tackle real business issues

Export led recovery

The government have said that they have incentivised Small & Medium Businesses with attractive corporation tax rates. They have justified this for two reasons. With the reduction in public sector spending the SMB sector is seen as the engine house of new jobs. They also recognise that growth and profitability will increase tax revenues.

With the UK economy experiencing very low current growth rates of 0.3%, growth within SMBs will only really come from an export led recovery!

UKTI statistics show where the worldwide growth is forecast to occur
70% of global growth in BRIC economies (Brazil, Russia, India and China)
30% of global growth in US
0% of global growth in EU!

With little or no growth anticipated in Europe, these economies are struggling and are unlikely to be the source of opportunities for new entrants. Enterprising businesses should be considering the potential offered by BRIC and US territories.

I am not saying every country will offer equal opportunities for all SMB's. Detailed research and investigation will be necessary to identify the potential. What works within your home market will need refining or reconfiguring to ensure it is both effective and competitive in a new market.

For example, I have recently started working with a Mumbai software product company who want to exploit the US market and they were looking for a Software Marketing Expert who could coach and mentor them in the product marketing and channel development strategies.

The challenge for me to enter that market was to reconfigure my service to make it an effective arms length solution where face to face meetings are not an option and Skype and email become the basis for all communication.

Chapter Five
Executive support to tackle real business issues

Business success achieved with Expert Coaching

New skills are not acquired in the classroom. Tiger Woods doesn't learn how to hit the ball 300 yards by studying text books. Wayne Rooney is not in the habit of sitting at a desk when developing on his natural ability to dart round defenders and score goals from 25 yards. No! They learn by practical exercise.

The same principle applies to business growth - there comes a time when you just have to leave the theory behind.

As a Software Sales and Marketing Coach I believe that learning 'on the job' develops the essential skills for a successful software business.

Just as Tiger and Wayne work with professional coaches, so a great software business is developed through coaching, Success can be achieved by sticking to some very simple rules.

Most businesses are started by an individual or partners who have the desire to be successful. Unfortunately the buffeting of the recession, the ongoing turmoil in Europe, the recent General Election and the imminent public sector cuts can dent those desires.

Developing the drive and discipline to focus the business can be the most challenging part of achieving success. You need to set business goals and identify the activities needed to meet those targets. These activities should include harnessing the power of social media, websites, and e-newsletters as well as modern sales techniques. Unfortunately many of these skills are not necessarily intuitive for technical based software businesses.

A great business coach can help you through this process and support your activities with practical experience and hands on assistance. This really works - believe me!

Chapter Five
Executive support to tackle real business issues

A "blueprint" for small business success.

Recent research conducted by the Warwick Business School suggests that there are tens of thousands of small UK businesses that are only a stone's throw away from making more profit that their peers.

The study outlines a 'blueprint for success' criteria which 43% of UK small and medium sized companies already follow. The study, commissioned by Royal Mail has identified six factors that have a "strong link" to above average trading performances in businesses that employ between 20-250 staff. In comparing and monitoring the growth rates amongst 500 businesses, the team of researchers found that those businesses already following three of the six key factors from the blueprint have reported sales growth of 17% from 2006 to 2009.

The six key factors for success are as follows;
- Striving for growth
- Managing flexibly
- People planning
- Marketing
- Research and development
- Process changes

Of the 500 businesses that participated in this research, 'Marketing' was considered to be a key factor in growth. The report stated that "Marketing is also important, with businesses adopting different strategies but those using broadcast media are seeing very significant benefits".

As a specialist Sales and Marketing Coach in the software sector, I am fully aware of the need to run successful e-marketing campaigns by harnessing the power of social media, websites, and e-newsletters. As the UK economy comes out of recession and into a period of growth it is more important now than ever that small to medium software businesses tackle the challenge of effectively marketing their products and services. As new opportunities emerge you need to be ready and primed with an effective marketing strategy.

Chapter Five
Executive support to tackle real business issues

Bring on the directors!

Software companies wanting to improve business performance should bring in non-executive directors to strengthen their Boards.

This advice comes from Software Sales and Marketing Coach, Terry Forsey who is advocating the introduction of 'non-execs' in his latest white paper that looks at the value of these individuals to the organisation.

"Research shows that business organisations with one or more non-executive directors typically perform better financially than those without," explained Terry. "These people can contribute critical skills that may be missing from the existing Board. When choosing people to fill these positions, it is important to select professionals with relevant experience and whose opinions are respected - the right non-exec can be a valuable asset."

"Non-exec Directors can be particularly useful to early stage businesses that are often operating in an environment that has lots of unknowns," continued Terry. "Whilst they do not carry a magic wand, they do bring experience and this can be invaluable when it comes to trading in difficult times."

One company that is successfully using a non-exec director is Halcyon Software of Peterborough, Managing Director, Lorraine Cousins said; "Since our non exec joined us, we have gone from being one of the 'also rans' to UK market leader in our field - we are the company that all our competitors now fear."

Another software business that concurs with this opinion is Alamein based in Beaconsfield.

"The figures speak for themselves!" said Director, Aston Clark. "Since our non-executive director joined our management team our sales have risen 50% and our wholesales and marketing functions are increasingly strategic, organised and professional. Our non-exec is a great asset and complements our 'techie' bias with no-nonsense commercial acumen.

Chapter Five
Executive support to tackle real business issues

If only... an avoidable tragedy.

I recently signed a new customer who had spent over 12 months developing their own in house software to help sell their consultancy services.

Their background was that they were a reseller of an American solution which didn't fully suit the European market. When the American software authors showed little appetite to make the necessary amendments they decided to recruit a developer and write it for specifically for this market.

This was the start of a rude awakening as they struggled to button down the functionality, allowed deadlines to slip, created a good looking website but with poor content and it became a horror story of incomplete projects. Throughout all this they allowed themselves to take their eye of the ball and their sales pipeline began to dry up.

At this point the MD, Geoff (not his real name) saw one of my adverts on LinkedIn and invited me in to have a look at what they were doing and recommend how to bring some stability and focus to their business.

I was concerned about the ability to afford my services when the business was so weak and was assured they had held back funding for help and assistance and had the full support of their bank. We planned our first meeting for a Monday afternoon.

A couple days before the planned meeting I made my customary call to the Geoff to confirm our arrangements and shared a joke about the then hung parliament. Everything felt good.

On Monday morning I received a call from a distraught Geoff to say that the Bank had just pulled the plug on their funding and all their hard work and personal investment was in tatters. I felt devastated for him. I really believe I could have helped him.

Geoff said "I know you could have been good for us. If only I'd found you sooner!" That hurt for three reasons,

I had only recently started experimenting with LinkedIn advertising. If I had done so sooner I might now have a happy customer;

Geoff has allowed himself to get too deep into the problem and had no release valve of a colleague, friend or trusted advisor to turn to. If he did have someone, he'd not have been in the mess he was in; and most importantly the bank who pulled the plug was RBS majority owned by the Tax payer and still paying big bonuses to the bankers who destroyed Geoff's business.

Chapter Five
Executive support to tackle real business issues

I was left feeling frustrated for people like Geoff who leave it too late to turn for professional advice and guidance. He'd never developed a software package before nor had his developer. He wouldn't have built a house without an architect yet took a chance on writing a software package without expert guidance. I know I lost a customer but Geoff ended up losing his company! A true tragedy yet avoidable!

Chapter Five
Executive support to tackle real business issues

Chapter Six
Case Studies

Chapter Six
Case Studies

The Client: Halcyon Software

Halcyon Software is an established software company with more than 20 years experience in systems management. Halcyon develops monitoring and automation software for IBM midrange computers as well as Windows, Linux, UNIX, AIX and Netware platforms. Large multinational companies, corporate data centres, as well as small to medium sized businesses use Halcyon Software products to proactively manage and automate their IT operations.

The Head Office is based in Peterborough, Cambridgeshire, and their software is used throughout the world with distributors in Europe, Australia and the USA. Customers include Digica, Capgemini, Avon Cosmetics, Honda, Raleigh, Burberry, Early Learning Centre, Arcadia and Budget Insurance, British Sugar, Volvo and Cummins Information Systems.

The Task
In 2002, Halcyon Software appointed Terry Forsey to review the way their business operated, in particular the need to develop and deliver an effective Sales and Marketing Strategy.

Halcyon recognised that their key strengths were in writing and developing sophisticated software and providing excellent technical customer support, but with a very limited Sales and Marketing function they acknowledged a significant requirement for expertise in this area.

"I think it is fair to say that it was with some degree of scepticism that I engaged Terry Forsey, having tried Consultants in the past to very little effect. However, I am happy to say that I have been proved entirely wrong!" Lorraine Cousins, MD Halcyon Software, Peterborough.

The Solution
Terry undertook a review of the sales and marketing process from promotion and lead generation through to deal aiming specifically to improve the new business win rate, particularly in the UK.

1. A review of marketing materials
The first phase of the project involved a complete review of how Halcyon's marketing materials were used. This identified a need to reduce the amount of literature that was sent to Halcyon's customers in order to adopt a more targeted and effective approach to their marketing activities.

Following a successful review of Halcyon's marketing materials Halcyon asked Terry to turn his attentions to their product offerings.

2. Reorganisation of the Halcyon product offering
It became clear to Terry that in order for Halcyon to differentiate themselves from their competitors and become more strategic in targeting specific markets Halcyon needed to reorganise their product offerings.

This led to the concept of bundling software into a 'family' of product suites enabling Halcyon to tailor their solutions to have broader appeal to both potential and existing customers. These new product suites delivered significant benefits to customers enabling Halcyon to provide more targeted and relevant software for diverse IT operations across all vertical sectors of the marketplace.

"In reorganising our products into suites, Terry made an enormous difference in a very short time." Lorraine Cousins, MD Halcyon Software, Peterborough.

Terry created a marketing positioning statement for Halcyon as "Experts in Multi-Platform Systems Management". He also created a positioning statement for each of the four product suites moving from the entry level product through to the flagship of the range.

To support the new product suites Terry re-worked the Halcyon Sales Proposal framework and took responsibility for managing the recruitment of a sales team.

"Terry is a highly professional sales and marketing coach - but he is far more than that. Add to this his mentoring capabilities, his ability to drill down to the critical issues and his inventive way of enabling you to solve them - and you have a very powerful force on your side." Lorraine Cousins, MD Halcyon Software, Peterborough.

3. Moving from direct selling to channel selling
The repositioning of Halcyon's products enabled them to attract larger more profitable customers which dramatically increased their average selling price.

The acquisition of larger customers created the need to review Halcyon's routes to market which led to the adoption of a new channel strategy using strategic partners to compliment Halcyon's Direct Sales.

Terry's expertise was utilised to support the creation of this dedicated channel strategy which culminated in successfully expanding the network of resellers and distributors in Europe, Australia and the US.

4. International Territory Gain
The expansion into new territories provided Halcyon with the opportunity to shift their reliance on UK & Europe market revenues and consider opportunities to set up subsidiaries in new territories.

In 2006 Halcyon successfully set up a subsidiary in Australia. In 2010 Australia is in line to achieve the revenue targets set by Halcyon in their business plan.

"Terry has helped us transform our business by helping us put in place winning strategies and manage the challenges of real growth. His style is good humoured, friendly, supportive and pragmatic, and he always delivers on time." Carole Chandler, Sales and Marketing Director Halcyon Software, Peterborough.

Following on from their success in Australia, Halcyon took a huge but vital step in opening a subsidiary in the USA to support activities and revenues being delivered by their established US reseller network. The US office drives sales through marketing initiatives with their channel partners. This subsidiary was opened just as the credit crisis hit in 2008. With America gradually emerging from the recession, Halcyon are already seeing an increase in sales from this subsidiary.

The Outcome

Terry's Appointment as Non-Executive Director.

Since 2002, Halcyon has grown significantly and experienced many successes with the help of Terry's expert mentoring and coaching skills. As Lorraine Cousins MD, commented,

"Since Terry joined us we have gone from being one of the "also rans" to UK market leader in our field - we are the company that all our competitors now fear."

In 2006 Terry was appointed Non-Executive Director for Halcyon where he is now involved in all of the monthly operational Board meetings and quarterly strategic GAP (Grow and Prosper) Committee meetings.

Carole Chandler, Sales and Marketing Director, Halcyon Software, Peterborough summed up "As Halcyon casts its net wider over international markets, Terry continues to help us to focus on versatile ways of creating revenues and developing future strategies".

Chapter Six
Case Studies

The Client: Alamein

Alamein, based in Berkshire, provide intelligent mobile data solutions to meet the challenges of today's mobile workplace. Using satellite navigation and tracking technology Alamein offer the most comprehensive range of mobile solutions to fleet operators today including data despatch solutions, online bookings and fleet management systems.

With customers in the UK and internationally, Alamein solutions keep organisations in control of their mobile workforces delivering optimized fleet efficiency and improved customer service.

The Challenge
After establishing the business in late 2000 and appointing key Partners as Solution Providers, Alamein embarked on acquiring a customer base that would deliver a strong revenue stream and profitable recurring revenues, typically from the passenger transport and courier sector of the market. As their business grew the co founders Aston Clarke and Douglas Kearney recognised that in order to achieve their goals they couldn't just rely on their core competences of technical expertise and partner relationships. They recognised that Alamein required a stronger sales and market presence in order to succeed.

In 2006 Alamein contacted Terry and for his assistance in helping them set up their Sales / Business Development function and define a strategy that would deliver sales from lead generation through to fulfilment.

The Solution
Terry was appointed to support Alamein initially over a 12 month period on this project which he delivered in two phases.

The first phase focused on establishing a strong sales resource which had the capability to deliver the required growth in sales. This included managing the recruitment process of Alamein's sales function by briefing recruitment consultants, defining the sales role, advising on remuneration levels and defining sales targets. Once a salesman was appointed Terry worked with the Directors to develop and monitor a 12 month business plan to achieve their goals, advising on any specific sales opportunities over the duration of the project.

To support the new sales function and ensure they were equipped to succeed Terry proposed a 12 month Marketing Plan with the key objective of generating leads and building credibility to ensure Alamein was on the radar of larger more profitable organisations. Within this second phase was the provision of collateral such as brochures, web content, presentations etc.

After the first 12 months Aston Clarke, Managing Director of Alamein commented on the achievements, "The figures speak for themselves! Since Terry joined our management team our sales have risen 50% and our whole sales and marketing function is increasingly strategic, organised and professional."

The Next Steps

The support that Terry provided to Alamein continues, with Terry being retained as Sales and Marketing Non Exec within their business. Over the last 3 years Alamein has doubled in size and they are now better equipped to achieve larger and more strategic sales. Terry not only gets involved internally but also represents Alamein in strategic negotiations and is a valued member of the Alamein Executive Team.

Terry has contributed to the company strategy and direction which now sees Alamein competing for business in a much wider market which includes patient transfer, community transport and freight logistics. Alamein are strengthening their product range via product suites and bespoke solutions to meet the requirements of larger and more diverse operators within the mobile market place.

"Terry is a great asset and complements our 'techie' bias with no-nonsense commercial acumen," concluded Aston Clarke, Alamein.

Chapter Six
Case Studies

The Client: FSI

FSI FM Solutions supply building services and facilities management software and are UK market leaders in Computer Aided Facilities Management (CAFM) for the FM Market. As part of their growth plan they conceived MMB Software Ltd a new venture planned for launch in 2010. MMB (Manage My Business) is charged with delivering a new hosted solution, TaskAdviser. This solution will be positioned at entry level end, as an easy to use web based application, available on a 'pay as you go' monthly fee per user basis for smaller businesses.

The business model will offer a low price, entry level solution on a monthly fee per user and seek to drive incremental revenues through the addition of further modules and services.

The primary business driver for this solution is the need for smaller businesses to improve their professional image when tendering for contracts and dramatically improve the speed and accuracy of customer invoicing.

The Challenge
FSI FM Solutions new business venture started in February 2010 with a new General Manager, Kevin Shipp coming on board. Kevin has experience working with some of the industry's leading companies including ADT Fire & Security Plc and Johnson Controls. 'TaskAdviser' from MMB Software Ltd was expected to be fully ready for a live start towards the end of March 2010. The initial challenge was to develop the strategy to bring this new solution to market on time.

TaskAdviser aimed to be the UK's first online Task Management System which organises a business and allows greater visibility and more control over people, customers, cash flow and costs. The business benefits of TaskAdviser were clear - speeding up administration, reducing paperwork and allowing small business owners more time to expand and improve their business.

With FSI's experience in larger more corporate solutions, it was not clear how to develop the strategy to bring this new solution to market and successfully launch it in 2010.

The Solution
With a considerable amount of experience working with many "pay as you go" and "on line" solutions Terry was able to bring his experience of a number of different sectors and solutions to help MMB build the following for TaskAdviser.

Agree an effective Positioning of TaskAdviser based on the target businesses within this market place; Identify a Market Engagement Model and Sales Engagement Process which would be effective in a high volume lower value Business to Business market place.

Chapter Six
Case Studies

Determine an effective Marketing Activity Plan;
Verify a pricing model for launch, ongoing sales and incorporating pricing bundles to deliver increased value and higher per customer revenues;
Advise on commercial and legal issues including licensing and service delivery terms and conditions.

Kevin Shipp General Manager of MMB Limited reported that" Terry has really helped me come to terms with the world of software and the internet. He has provided practical advice and been very supportive throughout this process."

Next Steps
With TaskAdviser successfully launched in early May 2010, Terry continues to work with the team to advice on any post launch issues and on the continued growth of the solution.

Compton Darlington, Business Development Director of FSI concluded "Terry has provided us with some key contributions at crucial stages of the launch of TaskAdviser providing practical and constructive solutions".

Chapter Six
Case Studies

The Client: Property Portfolio Software

Property Portfolio Software was founded by experienced landlord, author and public speaker Amer Siddiq, owner of Tax Portal Ltd. and creator of the Property Tax Portal website.

Amer has been investing in property since 1999. As his own property portfolio expanded, he began to search for a software solution that would assist him in managing his properties. Soon realising there was no software that offered a single suitable solution for managing a complete portfolio of properties, Amer, a very successful software designer himself, designed his own tool. Property Portfolio Software - "Landlords Property Manager" would enable landlords to overcome five of the biggest property management challenges faced by growing portfolios:

- Getting better organised: cutting the time spent handling paperwork
- Staying legal: keeping track of safety certificates and legal documents
- Tenant Management: making sure tenants get the information they need
- Income Tax Management: knowing what is due and when
- Maintaining and growing a positive cash-flow.

The Challenge
With over one million private landlords in the UK, Property Portfolio Software was very aware of an outstanding opportunity to dramatically grow their existing software sales and significantly increase the recurrent revenues from these sales.

In 2008 the software was already selling well through Google advertising and e-marketing to a database of 28,000 subscribers of the Property Tax Portal. The challenge was to drive increased sales of software by improved marketing activity beyond the internet, combining this activity with developing and releasing new products. This would take the business to another level and offer significant potential for growth.

In 2008 Property Portfolio Software contacted Terry for his help in exploring and overcoming the challenges of business growth and success.

The Solution
Working with Property Portfolio Software, Terry developed a 2008 Strategic Support Programme that would achieve the following objectives:

Understand the marketing opportunity for Property Portfolio Software
Develop a strategic marketing plan to take advantage of the identified opportunity.

Activities within this Strategic Support Programme included;

Chapter Six
Case Studies

Face to face meetings to gather information and understand the team's view of the opportunity,
Market research to clarify the target profile and determine the market potential,

- Identification of product developments,
- Recommendation of alternative pricing model and
- Recommendation of an annual marketing plan

The results were documented within a UK strategic plan and agreed with Amer. After three months of activity on this plan the outcome was formally reviewed and refinements were made to this plan.

After successfully executing the Strategic Support Programme, Amer Siddiq, Managing Director of Property Portfolio Software said of Terry,
"He works hard for your business and makes you work hard. He has helped us to successfully re-brand our business and understand what our real target market is. Terry helped us to put together a challenging marketing plan which has delivered excellent results"

Over the next twelve months, Property Portfolio Software experienced good business growth. Software sales increased by over 25%, a new website was launched, they ranked number one in Google search engine results for their primary key words and successfully developed some very valuable landlord and on-line partnerships with key landlord and legal associations.

The Next Steps
Property Portfolio Software have continued to work with Terry Forsey and, by the end of 2009, they were clearly recognised as the market leader in Landlords Software in the UK. Specifically this included:

- The only recognised supplier of the National Landlords Association
- The Official landlord software supplier of the Residential Landlords Association
- Strategic online partners with Landlord Zone and Lawpack

Despite tough market conditions, 2010 sees the potential for Property Portfolio Software to continue to grow. New product developments will continue to increase customer choice and market penetration, and new strategic partnerships are being developed to consolidate the market leading position of Property Portfolio Software.

Amer Siddiq, Managing Director closes "Terry has helped us think and behave like the market leader so it's no surprise that this is what we have become!"

Chapter Six
Case Studies

The Client: Triton Consulting

Triton Consulting, Information Management Specialists, formed in 1996. The highly experienced Triton consultants are able to advise on the full range of IBM Information Management Solutions, in particular DB2 for z/OS, DB2 for LUW, IBM Optim and DB2 Connect. The Triton owners and directors have a wealth of expertise in the DB2 arena as well as many years experience of providing high end technical leadership on large application development projects.

Since Triton Consulting was formed the company has gone from strength to strength, in 1998 becoming a Premier Business Partner of IBM, Business Partner of EDS/HP and in 2007 they were awarded Value Added Reseller for Business Objects.

Over the last decade Triton have expanded beyond consultancy and now offer a range of services. Working extensively and successfully across a number of different market sectors, Triton now offers a Remote DBA Managed Service and DB2 education services.

The Challenge
Triton's technical abilities and expertise have enabled them to build exceptional technical relationships with customers. As a team Triton are technically strong with a capable reputation. In the past this has resulted in a high level of referral business.

Outside of the business Triton won through referrals and recommendations, they had real difficulties winning new business. When Triton first met with Terry Forsey in 2007 they were having problems in the sales process, in particular when engaging at Director and Senior Manager Decision-maker level. As a smaller business, Triton wanted to target two mutually exclusive segments with independent routes to market.

At this point in time there were limited out bound marketing campaigns that might identify potential opportunities to target these sectors for sales leads. Terry advised that they should revisit their business engagement model, to reconsider what they are selling and to whom. This would be followed by a review of the lead generation process and sales engagement process.

The key focus for Triton was to generate more leads and convert them into profitable business.

The Solution
Terry led a Triton Non-Executive Support Programme working closely with the Directors to review the whole customer engagement model and help them to really understand who their customers are and how to effectively engage them. From this they have developed a continuous process of improving the skills of sales and marketing resources, the effectiveness of the sales and marketing function and the overall focus and profitability of the business.

Chapter Six
Case Studies

The Outcome

In the past Lead Generation was driven by the Sales Function. Today, this is no longer the case as they have recruited an experienced marketing manager who has successfully harnessed effective communications through regular e-newsletters, promotional campaigns, website improvements, blogs and the effective use of Twitter.

The Sales function, now with a vastly improved monitoring and reporting process has adopted a more effective consultative selling approach replacing the previous transactional selling method.

Terry continues to work closely with Triton Consulting on regular sales and marketing operational meetings, quarterly business strategic planning and an annual business review. Julian Stulher, Director Triton Consulting, Welwyn Garden City said that, "As consultants ourselves, we're very aware of the impact that good strategic advice can have on a business. Terry's expert guidance has been a critical factor in the successful transformation of our sales and marketing area."

As a result Triton has grown through a recession and can see a stronger more diverse future. Of the overall business improvements, Paul Stoker, Director, Triton Consulting, Welwyn Garden City concluded, "With Terry's help and expertise, Triton has become much better managed and more successful. We now have a stronger shared purpose with a much greater understanding of business goals and our strategic direction."

Chapter Six
Case Studies

The Client: ITAZ

ITAZ, a Mumbai software publisher is a very successful provider of Document Management solutions to medium businesses, Corporates and Government departments. Their Globodox solution is marketed worldwide and is being utilised by organisations such as Department of Justice (USA), Thermo Fisher Scientific (UK) and Hutchison Telecommunications (Sri Lanka). Globodox is available directly from ITAZ's web site and internationally via local and national resellers.

Globodox has achieved impressive sales growth aided by businesses looking for a more cost effective fully featured off the shelf solution that has enabled them to manage their documents more efficiently.

In 2008 following the success of Globodox ITAZ launched Sohodox, a Small Business Document Management Solution designed to specifically meet the needs of smaller businesses. Sold exclusively through the web the Sohodox solution has achieved very encouraging initial sales across the US market, indicating a high demand for such a product.

Shiraz Ahmed, Chief Executive Officer, ITAZ, felt that their business had great growth potential but knew that he needed to tap into the experience of a successful software marketer in order to help them achieve the next level of company growth.

ITAZ were used to working with outsourced service providers, but not always satisfied with the level of service and delivery they received. They had experienced a very common scenario where senior consultants would present and sell a service, whilst junior less capable practitioners were given the delivery task.

Shiraz, wanted to work with a consultancy where the knowledge and experience of the consultant led the delivery of all projects.

ITAZ had two goals. The first was to improve the worldwide marketing of Globodox. They sought to increase the level of their international presence. In particular ITAZ were very keen to learn how to effectively drive their channel presence and develop good local reseller relationships.

Their second goal was to reach a wider global audience with Sohodox and target specific niche sectors. ITAZ knew they would have to dramatically improve their web marketing activities, by advertising and maintaining a stronger presence through social media websites.

For these reasons ITAZ decided to seek a Software Marketing Expert who had a strong web presence and could help them penetrate the international market place both through resellers and on the web.
As Shiraz pointed out, "Mumbai is very strong in software services, yet surprisingly there are only a few local marketing consultants with international

software product marketing experience. For this reason I had to look further afield for another consultancy. I was particularly impressed with the strong web presence and excellent testimonials of Terry Forsey Consulting. Terry seemed to have just the track record we were seeking having spent many years working in software sales and marketing. He also had the international experience we were looking for, working in UK, Europe and across US markets"

One of the early challenges for this new working partnership was to get to grips with delivering all services exclusively over the web using Skype for each meeting. Terry felt the lack of face to face meetings early could be particularly challenging. However, both parties were committed to making it work and have easily overcome this. All regular meetings take place using Skype and the working relationship between Terry and ITAZ is one that grows stronger from meeting to meeting.

An early win for ITAZ was a very strong product review of the Sohodox product on CNET. This has further strengthened the download pipeline and puts ITAZ in a very strong position.

Shiraz, is positive about the future but not complacent, he went on to say, "There's lots of work to be done still, but working with Terry means we are extremely well placed to use his ideas and experience to make the right decisions and short cut many obstacles."

Chapter Six
Case Studies

The Client: DWS

DWS provide software development expertise and support to companies who want to customise and extend JDEdwards EnterpriseOne. Formed in 1998 and a JD Edwards Certified Advantage Partner, DWS has built an enviable reputation as a true consulting expert in JD Edwards development.

DWS offer bespoke upgrade services to JD Edwards users. DWS have built a reputation for seamlessly identifying upgrade requirements and delivering solutions to legacy JD Edwards software systems.

The Challenge
After many years of experience in upgrading customers' E1 systems to higher release levels, DWS recognised the need to expand their services based around automating the estimation and upgrade process. These would be based upon their Dimension software, which automatically scans every line of code to precisely identify all modifications and enable an accurate fixed price upgrade.

To help refine their proposition, maximise their exposure and achieve market penetration, DWS appointed Terry to review all aspects of marketing and selling DWS Dimension.

The Solution
Terry was appointed to undertake a comprehensive review of Sales and Marketing for DWS Dimension and recommend changes, which would result in an improved operation and growth in revenue.

Terry worked with DWS as part of an Executive Support Programme; a significant part of this support programme was to review the sales engagement process. This identified that, in order for DWS to differentiate themselves and deliver increased value to their customers, a new range of fixed price services should be developed around the Dimension software.

This range of fixed priced services included:
- Scoping and Estimating service;
- Undertaking the upgrade with DWS resources;
- Supporting service for in-house upgrades;
- Optimisation services; and
- Ongoing support services.

The project was completed within a critical time frame as the new services, the supporting collateral and a new website had to be completed to ensure a successful launch of this new range of services at the UKOUG (UK Oracle User Group) Annual JD Edwards Conference.

Barry Burke, MD, reported, "During the conference, we were very successful in uncovering several opportunities, two of which signed up for our services.

These two deals in particular present additional opportunities for DWS services,"

The Outcome

In the run up to the launch of the new range of DWS Dimension services at the JD Edwards Conference, DWS were awarded the 'UKOUG Innovation Partner of the Year 2009/2010' for DWS Dimension, an award that Barry Burke, MD was very proud to accept on behalf of the DWS team.

Barry Burke, MD said of the project, "Engaging the services of Terry Forsey was a good move for DWS. Terry brought a great deal of insight and professionalism to our marketing efforts and wasn't afraid to challenge the status quo. I would happily recommend him to other likeminded IT companies.' Barry concluded that, "As a result of this work, today we have the most complete range of fixed price upgrade services in the JD Edwards market."

Chapter Six
Case Studies

How Terry Forsey Consulting can help

Successfully turning software into profit.

Terry Forsey Consulting is a specialist Sales and Marketing Consultancy helping smaller software businesses run successful marketing campaigns and grow their sales and their profits! In short, to win more customers. We provide high value services to small to medium-sized software companies, working successfully with a range of clients helping them to grow their business.

Terry Forsey has spent over 30 years working as a Sales & Marketing focused Director within the Software Industry. His experience has been with Small and Medium sized software companies where he has repeatedly wrestled with the challenges of growth and survived three previous recessions!

Terry has been part of a management team that has raised Venture Capital on three occasions and sold businesses twice. He narrowly averted a complete disaster when a major client called in the receiver over the Christmas Holidays. An experience he describes as "one of the most focusing events of my career!" Terry is pleased to announce that after two years this business was successfully sold.

Since 2002, Terry has been a Sales and Marketing consultant helping small owner managed software businesses build successful sales and marketing activities and achieve significant growth. Terry was recently described (unprompted) as the "Affordable John Harvey-Jones".

Terry Forsey Consulting offers a range of services that can help to boost your sales and profitability –

Selling Software – Helping your sales team to be more effective and win business.

Software Marketing –helping you through the challenges of marketing your products and services and, most importantly, generating leads.

Executive Coaching & Mentoring – Individual support to help tackle today's issues.

Non-Executive Services – providing an independent view of the company that is removed from day-to-day running.

As a Software Sales and Marketing expert, Terry understands firsthand the challenges that small and medium-sized owner managed software businesses face – more importantly he knows how to overcome them to create a successful business. In addition to our services, Terry is a regular producer of white papers to address the challenges that many small software companies face. These are available to registered website visitors.

Glossary of Terms

A

Account	a specific customer who is buying your product or services
Added Value	increasing the attractiveness of a product / service/ process etc to a customer which encourages a sales decision based on something other than price. Added values can be real or perceived. A competent and informed Sales person can often be seen as the added value to secure a sale.
Advantages	an element of a product or service that makes it better than others, especially the one of the incumbent supplier or that of a competitor
Advertorial	an advertisement written in an editorial style promoting the benefits of a specific organisation, product or service
Affiliate	an organisation that has some form of relationship with another eg. Minority share, sales and marketing interests etc
Affiliate marketing	a marketing practice whereby one organisation rewards their affiliates for each customer, lead or sale brought to them by the affiliates marketing efforts
Affiliate network	a group of affiliates that support a businesses marketing efforts
Appointment	see sales appointment

B

Banner Ad	a form of web advertising, whereby the advertisers advert is embedded on a web page
Benefits	the gain that a customer derives from a specific product, solution or service
Blog	is a shared on-line diary often used as a marketing PR tool for high profile individuals within organisations
Brand	a brand is the identity of a product, service or company and is reflected in a companies values and the experience received by a customer or buyer. Brand is reflected in all customer touch points i.e. messages, point of sale, customer service, advertising, staff etc.
Business operations	are those ongoing recurring activities involved in the running of a business for the purpose of producing value for the stakeholders.
Business strategy	a long term plan of action designed to achieve a particular goal or set of goals or objectives
Buyer	person responsible for procurement
Buying Signal	a point where a buyer indicates they are favourably considering or have made the

Glossary of Terms

decision to buy. These signals are not always obvious and are often missed by sales people.

C

Call to action — a statement usually found near the conclusion of a commercial message that urges the consumer / reader to act. Usually in relation to purchasing, reading, contacting or downloading something

Call centre — a centralised operation where a group of individuals manage calls for the purpose of sales, customer service etc.

Caption — a short explanation, description or heading

Channel — a route to market either directly or indirectly via resellers or distributors

Channel marketing — marketing programs targeted to appeal to the differing channel partners

Chartered Institute of Marketing — The Chartered Institute of Marketing (CIM) is a professional marketing body based in UK with over 50,000 members worldwide. Based in Cookham near Maidenhead, CIM offers professional development to marketing practitioners across the world

Circulation — an average number of copies distributed / readership

Click through Rate — a metric that helps show how your ads are performing. The number of ad clicks / number of impressions x 100

Closing — the point at which a negotiation or deal is finalised

CNET — *CNET* is a website for tech product reviews, news, price comparisons, free software downloads, daily videos, and podcasts.

Coach — a professional who uses their experience and knowledge to develop and improve the business skills of others

Collaboration — a method in which the sales person or organisation really collaborates with the customer to help them reach a buying decision

Cold call — the first call or meeting with a prospective customer without an appointment

Competitor — a company in the same industry or similar which offers a similar product or service which address common problems

Commodity — a product or service which has become mass produced, widely available, easy to make, de-mystified and simplified. Commoditised products are generally mass-market and are suitable for large-scale distribution methods. Commoditised products are usually associated with a reduction

Glossary of Terms

	in costs, prices and profit margins
Compete	to position your business against another's to try to gain competitive advantage and win a sale
Competition	businesses that work within your trading environment and are competing for the same business
Consultative selling	a sales process whereby the seller provides material insights and knowledge of the buyer's business and demonstrates value to secure the sale
Conversion	converting a sales lead or prospect to a customer
Copyright	"Copyright is a set of exclusive rights granted to the author or creator of an original work, including the right to copy, distribute and adapt the work." **Definition taken from Wikipedia, the free encyclopaedia**
Cost efficiency	
Cost per enquiry	a metric by which a cost is attributed to the marketing efforts required to generate an enquiry or lead
Cost per thousand (CPM)	a measurement for the advertising costs paid per thousand impressions in web advertising
CRM	Customer Relationship Management – a term used for the processes involved in managing customer activity both pre and post sale
Customer	any individual or organisation who purchases your product or solution
Customer database	the collation of specific customer details for an organisations total number of customers. Frequently used for sales, marketing and customer service activities
Customer Relationship Management (see CRM)	See CRM
D	
Deal	a colloquial term referring to the trading terms or agreement between buyer and seller. Generally this term is not used in a professional situation.
Decision maker	the person in the prospect organisation who has the power and budgetary authority to agree a sale or proposal
Demographics	groupings of people defined by specific characteristics for marketing purposes eg. Age, sex, geography, wealth, interests etc
Differentiation	a method of positively positioning a product / service or business in an alternative way to the competition for commercial gain
Direct mail	the practice of sending marketing materials

Glossary of Terms

	directly to a target audience, usually via print or or postal service
Direct marketing	Marketing and promotional activities targeted directly at the end user e.g. Telesales, direct mail etc
Distribution	the breadth of coverage for a particular product or solution either directly or via resellers. Understanding and establishing the best distribution models 'routes to market' are a critical aspect of any business, they are influenced by many factors and may change over time as a businesses product, the market and technology evolves.
Download.com	Download.com is an internet download directory website, launched in 1996 as a part of CNET
E	
E-Newsletter	a regular publication that is distributed electronically to opt in subscribers
Entrepreneur	a person who has possession of a new enterprise, venture or idea and assumes significant accountability for the inherent risks and the outcome
Escrow Agreement	a document that sets out how an end user accesses the purchased software code in the event that the software vendor is unable to fulfil it's obligations
E-Survey	a survey distributed electronically to opt in subscribers
Exclusivity agreement	an exclusive agreement usually between manufacturer and reseller , which often relates to the distribution of a product or service to give competitive advantage, usually for a specific period of time
Exit Page	the page that a visitor leaves a website
F	
FAB (see features, advantages, benefits)	See features, advantages, benefits
Features	a prominent characteristic of a product or solution
Features and benefits	a sales and marketing practice used to convince buyers/ end users to purchase a product or solution by highlighting the key characteristics of that solution (features) and how these specific features benefit the user / meet their requirements.
Field sales	teams of individuals selling on a one to one basis usually to resellers
Forecast	See sales forecast
G	
Google AdWords	Google Adwords is Google's online advertising

Glossary of Terms

program. Adwords lets the user create, simple, effective ads and display them to people already searching online for information related to your business.

H

Headline	an attention grabbing statement at the top of an article or advertisement

I

Influencer	people within a prospect organisation who may not have the power to agree a sale or proposal but have the power to influence or persuade the decision maker.
Institute of Directors	the Institute of Directors (IoD) is a UK-based organisation, incorporated by royal charter in 1903 to support, represent and set standards for company directors. It occupies Grade I listed premises on Pall Mall, London
Inst of Sales & Mkt	The Institute of Sales & Marketing Management (ISMM) is the UK's only professional body for salespeople. Founded in 1911 to promote standards of excellence in sales and sales management and to enhance the status and profile of sales as a profession
Intangible	an asset that isn't materialistic or physical but offers great value eg. Software or Consultancy
Introduction	a sales lead / introduction to a potential customer via an already known / reputable source
Impression	the appearance of an online advertisement in search engines

J

K

L

Landing Page	the page your website visitors arrive at after clicking on a link
Lead	a prospect customer usually from a known or recommended source
Lead-time	the time between placing an order / advertisement etc and fulfilment
LinkedIn	LinkedIn is the business oriented social networking site with over 75 million members. It connects users to their trusted contacts and helps them exchange knowledge, ideas and opportunities with a broader network of professionals. LinkedIn is often used with other social networking and e-marketing tools to form an integrated social media strategy.

M

Glossary of Terms

Major account	a customer that delivers a significant revenue contribution to a business and is included in a companies overall strategic plan
Managing Director	a director of a company who has overall responsibility for its day-to-day operations.
Margin	difference between the cost price and selling price of a product. This figure is often illustrated as a % and can be expressed in gross (difference between cost and selling price) or net terms (after overheads are deducted).
Market research	the process of gathering, analysing and interpreting information about the market , a product or service
Market segmentation	the process of producing specific groupings of customers for marketing purposes based on specific characteristics
Market share	the percentage of sales within a specific market for any given business
Marketing channels	routes available to marketers to target end users e.g. Resellers, distributors, media etc
Marketing database	Database available to marketers for promotional purposes, often segmented for more targeted activities
Marketing Director	an individual who is responsible for the overall marketing function within an organisation
Marketing manager	an individual who is responsible for a specific area within the marketing function
Marketing mix	combination of marketing factors used when selling a product or service. Commonly known as the 4P's (product, place, price and promotion) and taken from Neil Borden's American Marketing Association presidential address in 1953.
Marketing strategy	A marketing strategy is a plan which identifies the marketing activities to support the overall company strategy and goals. It incorporates product development, promotion, distribution, price and positioning.
Mentor	a trusted, experienced professional who guides and counsels an individual with potential
N	
Negotiation	the process by which two parties agree commercial terms or resolve areas of dispute by trading concessions to arrive at situation that is acceptable to both parties ie.supplier and customer
Networking	a method of developing sales opportunities and contacts based on referrals and introductions –

Glossary of Terms

	either face to face at meetings, or via phone, email, business networking websites etc.
Non-Executive Director	a Non-Executive Director sits on the board of a company along side the Executive Directors. A Non-Executive Directors' role is to provide a creative contribution to the board by providing objectivity. Non-Executive Directors focus on board matters, thus providing an independent view of the company that is removed from day-to-day running.
O	
Objections	reasons given by a buyer as to why they are not prepared to purchase a product or service at that particular time / in it's current format / at these terms etc.
Objection handling	the art of managing and overcoming a buyers specific objections to secure a sale
Objectives - sales	a set of predefined tasks / targets / milestones on which a sales person is monitored
Open questions	a set of questions that do not illicit a 'yes' or 'no' answer. Open questions are designed to extract specific information from the customer to provide an accurate picture of their specific needs / requirements etc
Opt -In	express permission of a customer or recipient of a mail, email etc to allow a business / marketer to send them information / promotional messages etc. Direct marketers generally send regular messages until the recipient opts out.
P	
Page rank	page rank is the overall importance that Google assigns to the overall importance of a web page
Pain/Need/Challenge	a specific business issue or requirement that a customer needs resolving in order to achieve a sale
Pay per Click	Pay per Click advertising simply means paying to put a listing or advert for your website at, or near the top of the search engines. It is an online advertising payment model in which payment is based solely on qualifying click-throughs.
Pay per Download	a payment model whereby customers only pay per service or solution downloaded
Pay per Impression	online advertising payment model in which payment is based solely on the appearance of ads
Pay per lead (PPL)	
Positioning	refers to how a product / service or proposition is presented or marketed in relation to the market place.

Glossary of Terms

PR	Public Relations - ongoing activities to establish and promote a favourable relationship with potential customers
Press relations	process of communicating with the mass media
Product	an item, solution or service offered for sale
Proof	proof is when someone, other than you or your company, says something about your product, company, or service that helps to build trust and respect. Proof includes letters of recommendation from other customers, testimonials, case studies, lists of clients, third party studies, copies of articles from trade journals etc.
Proposal / sales proposal	usually a written offer from a sales organisation to a prospect customer detailing specific information regarding a potential sale. The sales proposal is part of the sales process and the content would typically include specifications, prices, terms and conditions, warranty details etc
Proposition	the offering put forward to a potential buyer which includes the product, price, margin, marketing support etc
Prospect	a potential customer before the sale is made
Q	
Questioning techniques	the process used to extract information from the potential customer to identify their specific needs
R	
Referral	the details of a potential customer supplied or recommended by an existing customer or contact
Retention	the process of retaining a customer to ensure maximum value
Return on investment	a performance measurement designed to measure the financial return / success of a specific marketing activity after costs have been deducted
Revenue	the amount of income generated from sales and services
Risk	Risk is a combination of the financial, social, emotional, and time costs that a company and individual decision-maker will bear as a result of making a mistake. Usually in relation to appointing a new supplier or increasing a product portfolio.
ROI	See return on investment
S	
Sales appointment	a meeting made between buyer and seller to discuss the potential to trade
Sales commission	the amount paid to an individual or a distributor / reseller for achieving a pre determined number of

Glossary of Terms

	sales
Sales contribution	See sales margin
Sales cycle	The time / process between the first contact with the customer to close of sale. Sales cycles vary depending on the complexity of the product being sold , current market conditions, size of organisation etc
Sales Director	an individual who is responsible for the overall sales function within an organisation
Sales forecast	a prediction of future sales, based mainly on past sales performance, the economic climate and planned marketing activities
Sales funnel	see sales pipeline
Sales influencer	an individual who isn't responsible for the final purchasing decision but contributes to it
Sales lead	see lead
Sales manager	an individual who is responsible for a specific area within the sales function
Sales management	is the process of managing an organisation's sales goals and encompasses the entire selling effort including planning, staffing, training, leading & motivating
Sales margin	See margin
Sales Pipeline	a tracking and monitoring mechanism to identify the status of a companies potential sales from initial lead generation status through to agreed sale
Sales Process	is a systematic approach to selling a product or service
Sales proposition	See proposition
Sales strategy	a sales strategy provides the framework and direction to enable an organisation to achieve it's sales targets and forms part of the overall company strategy. It is a planned approach to account-management, prospect identification and qualification, sales presentations, and order generation.
Sales Proposal	a document that provides a potential customer with enough information, persuasively presented, to prove your case and motivate the customer to buy your services or applications
Sales Proposition	a description of the sales activities, overall competitive positioning and summary of the propositions unique selling points
Segmentation	See market segmentation
Selection Criteria	a predetermined set of requirements, standards or processes which a potential customer uses to select a new supplier.

Glossary of Terms

SPIN selling ®	a sales technique developed by Neil Rackman that is designed for larger more complex sales and aims to develop rapport and understanding with the customer through questioning skills that focus on 4 types of questions : Situation questions, Problem questions, Implication questions, Need – pay off questions. ®*Note Neil Rackman copyright
Solution	product or service offering
Solution Selling	The process of developing a comprehensive understanding of the customer's business and industry, defining needs at a strategic level and offering solutions that will help the customer address their unique objectives.
Strategic selling ®	The term strategic selling is, however, frequently used and does not necessarily refer to the American Miller Heirman organisations specific training methods and materials. The term 'strategic selling' used in this document refers to a strategic method of selling whereby an organisation takes a more strategic approach to it's customers and undertakes a review of the potential customer's markets and their strategic priorities etc. Strategic Selling® is a registered and protected product name belonging to the American Miller Heirman training organisation.
T	
Tangible	an aspect of a product or service that can be seen or measured in terms of value and cost eg. warranties, installation, spare part etc
Targeting	selection of a group of customers to whom a business wants to sell or market their product to.
Telemarketing	the practice of marketing, promoting or surveying a product or service over the telephone
Telesales	the practice of selling a product or service over the telephone
Tender	the formal process of pitching for business following an invitation to do so, usually from a large organisation or government etc. Tenders require businesses to meet specific criteria and deadlines in order to qualify to be included in any potential sale pitch and generally form part of a lengthy process.
Territory	designated area for trading for specific customers, sales people etc
Transactional selling	the process of closing the order there and then and typically involves negotiation with the buyer on price with little interaction with others in the

Glossary of Terms

company.

Twitter	Twitter is a website, owned and operated by Twitter Inc., which offers a social networking and microblogging service . When used for business it enables users to stay connected, (via 'tweets' messages) to their customers and followers and allows them to share information, gather real-time market intelligence and feedback, and build relationships with people who are interested in their business. Twitter is often used with other social networking and emarketing tools to form an integrated social media strategy.

U

Unique selling point	See USP
USP	a real or perceived benefit of a product or service that sets a company apart from the competition in order to gain competitive advantage

V

Value	what you believe you receive for the price. It is a perception and is very subjective. It is not always quantifiable. Price invites competition. Value locks out the competition.
Vertical market	a targeted grouping of industries, customers or narrow segment of an industry that share similar characteristics and trading requirements, banking, financial services etc
Viral marketing	marketing that encourages people to pass on a marketing message, usually via email or the web

W

White Paper	an authoritative report or guide that addresses a specific business issues and how to manage it. White Papers are often used to support sales and marketing efforts establishing proof and credibility.